BUT FACTS EXIST

Thomas Freeman

BUT FACTS EXIST

An Enquiry
into Psychoanalytic Theorizing

Thomas Freeman

Foreword by

Brian Martindale

London
KARNAC BOOKS

First published in 1998 by
H. Karnac (Books) Ltd.
58 Gloucester Road
London SW7 4QY

British Library Cataloguing in Publication Data

A C.I.P for this book is available from the British Library

   ISBN 1 85575 193 3

10 9 8 7 6 5 4 3 2 1

Edited, designed, and produced by Communication Crafts

Printed in Great Britain by BPC Wheatons Ltd, Exeter

ACKNOWLEDGEMENTS

I wish to thank my wife for her constant support in the writing of this book—not least her correcting and typing the manuscript. I also wish to thank Dr Jessie Sym of Edinburgh for drawing my attention to Robert Burns' poem "The Dream". Finally I am indebted to Dr Paul Williams for sharing with me his interest in the evolutionary basis of Freud's psychoanalysis.

CONTENTS

ACKNOWLEDGEMENTS   v

FOREWORD *by Brian Martindale*   ix

Introduction   1

1   The clinical foundations of Freud's pleasure
    (unpleasure) principle   5

2   The theory of repression   19

3   Freud's theory of mind reformulated:
    Beyond the Pleasure Principle   31

4   The new schema of the mental apparatus
    and its antecedents   53

5   A short detour around Freud's theories of anxiety   71

6   The reinterpretation of clinical facts
     (descriptive data)   79

7   Psychoses and psychoanalytic theories
     of development   88

8   Theories of narcissistic object relations   100

9   On the formal aspects of psychotic phenomena   114

10   Theory and technique in psychoanalysis   123

11   Is there a way forward?   149

APPENDIX   159

REFERENCES   161

INDEX   173

FOREWORD

Brian Martindale

D r Thomas Freeman has had a long and distinguished career as a clinician, theoretician, author, and teacher. In his many publications he has demonstrated his profound knowledge of the evolving theories both of Freud and of later theoreticians. He is one of the few British psychoanalysts who has sustained extensive clinical contact with patients suffering from psychotic disorders as well as those with character disorders.

In this latest outstanding book, Freeman brings together these attributes of master clinician and theoretician with the aim of assisting mental health clinicians, researchers, and psychoanalysts in clarifying the clinical basis upon which psychoanalytic theories have been developed. In so doing, he also wishes to facilitate the important debate regarding whether core aspects of psychoanalysis and psychoanalytic theory belong within the natural sciences and to examine and question how closely differing psychoanalytic theories match clinical facts.

Readers of this book will find themselves highly stimulated by the way in which Freeman consistently addresses indisputable "clinical facts"—phenomena such as dreams, parapraxes, and psychotic phenomena that occur both independently and within the analytic relationship and that are verifiable through repeated observations independent of any one observer. Freeman uses extensive and vivid clinical material as his starting point. He carefully distinguishes between clinical facts and psychoanalytic facts, which emerge *only* in the patient–analyst relationship and are therefore not verifiable in the same way as clinical facts. In a most objective manner, Freeman then describes and debates in succeeding chapters major psychoanalytic theories that have been espoused to account for both clinical and psychoanalytic facts.

In chapter one, the clinical facts of dreams and the verbalizations of schizophrenic patients are used to look at how Freud arrived at his theories of the pleasure principle and wish-fulfilment to explain aspects of both the form and the content of such facts. Primary and secondary processes are clearly delineated. What is particularly important about this chapter is Freeman's capacity to demonstrate the continuing explanatory power of these early theories of Freud to these clinical phenomena.

Chapters two and three describe quite a number of clinical facts that Freud encountered that necessitated further theoretical developments. Freeman presents his own clinical material to demonstrate how the theory of repression came to assume major theoretical and therapeutic importance. He moves on to show how theories different from those of wish-fulfilment and the pleasure principle were necessary to explain repetitive mental phenomena and their buried connections with recent or long-past traumatic experiences. A highlight of chapter three is Freeman's discussion of Freud's own tentativeness concerning his theory of the death instinct as a contributing explanation of the clinical facts of repetition phenomena. He gives detailed clinical material to support alternative theories (of Freud) that Freeman believes are closer to empirical data.

In chapter four, Freeman outlines Freud's revisions of theory contained in the structural model that were intended to encompass the vicissitudes of internal and external object relations. Clinical facts demonstrated the vagaries of processes of identification and sexual identification in the ego and superego in such phenomena as narcissism, delusional jealousy, depression, group psychology, and psychosis. It is made clear that Freud continued to observe that wish-fulfilment and defensive reactions to these played a major role within the developing structural theory of the mental apparatus. Towards the end of this chapter, Freeman returns to Freud's incorporation of the dual instinct theory (life and death instincts) within his theory of superego functioning. He suggests that both for Freud and for some subsequent theoreticians it was a lack of therapeutic success that led to revised theoretical formulations (in Freud's case, his emphasis on the death instinct), but that these revisions did not always fit the clinical facts as well as earlier theories had.

In chapter five, Freeman discusses Freud's evolving theories of anxiety and suggests that Freud may have erred when he considered completely rejecting his economic theory of anxiety. Dr Freeman thinks that there may be qualitative differences between the nature of the anxiety displayed in some mental disorders and the signal anxiety experienced by healthy persons in the face of real dangers. As always, clinical material is given in this case to support the retaining of the possibility of a libidinal economic explanation for some cases of anxiety.

At this point in the book, Freeman begins to make some cogent points that he believes underlie much confusion and debate about psychoanalytic theory. In chapter six, he particularly focuses on the concept of splitting, which has acquired such a central place in many object relation theories—such as those of Klein, Fairbairn, and Bion—that extend Freud's structural theories, in which the dual instinct theory was so central. However, for Freeman, the concept of splitting has tended to exclude totally Freud's earlier ideas of the role of wish-fulfilment, repression, and primary process activity. Splitting (as an ego activity) has become a central explanation that has in some theories completely overtaken its initial use as a description. These explanations have involved a fresh interpretation of clinical phenomena, replacing such earlier concepts as repression.

He then reviews the psychoanalytic theories of very early mal-development—especially those of Abraham, Klein, and Fairbairn—that have developed from studying the clinical features of adult psychosis. He provides evidence suggesting that great caution is needed in extrapolating from the clinical facts of a current psychosis to claims that the problems had existed in identical form in the early months of infancy, as is implied in the theories and choice of terminology used by these theoreticians. Clinical material is presented that demonstrates the complexities of the issues that are often marginalized by the theory.

In chapter eight, Freeman carefully maps out the different theories of narcissistic object relations, concentrating on those of Freud, Klein and her followers, and Kohut. He emphasizes that the unitary theory of Kohut dispenses with theories of pathological narcissism that regard such phenomena as having defensive functions against anxieties that might be caused by phantasies and affects. Schizoid mechanisms relating to the death instinct are at at the core of Klein's theory, rejecting libido theory, with its redistribution of libidinal cathexes from object to self. Freeman highlights important differences in clinical opinion regarding whether nonpsychotic and psychotic narcissistic disturbances are different qualitatively or merely quantitatively. The theories of pathological narcissism are incompatible with the concept of a psychopathological continuity between psychotic and non-psychotic narcissistic disorders.

Freeman's extensive experience with psychotic disorders comes through exceptionally well in his discussion of the various theories of the formal aspects of psychotic disorders in chapter nine. He outlines these theories and points out their incompatibility with one another. He then delineates his own ideas connected with Freud's theories of dreams, which, he feels, offer a better model as to how reality testing is lost. He is also of the opinion that the various dynamic theories espoused do not include an economic component, which, he believes, needs to be considered if one is to understand remissions and the effectiveness at times of psychopharmacological treatments.

Turning, in chapter ten, to technique, Freeman sketches the history of technique and the way in which it has shifted back and forth between being led by empirical procedures and theoretical deductions based on the data produced. The different functions and roles of the analyst in treatment are described according to the different major contemporary theories of psychopathology. Freeman believes, along with others such as Wallerstein, that the clinical evidence is that schizophrenic and dysmorphophobic patients' responsiveness to full or modified psychoanalytic treatment is not dependent on a specific treatment technique or theory. From his clinical experience, he concludes that it is related to the patient's capacity or lack of it to make an attachment with the analyst, irrespective of the interpretative technique or theory.

In the final chapter, Freeman questions whether there is a way forward in testing out different and sometimes diametrically opposed psychoanalytic theories of clinical phenomena and maintaining psychoanalysis as a subject conforming to scientific criteria. Perhaps his answer is encompassed in the whole tone of his book, which conveys a central focus on clinical facts and phenomena and a refreshing open-mindedness to examine all theories derived from such phenomena for evidence as to whether they fit the clinical facts. His open-mindedness includes evidence from non-psychoanalytic findings and other forms of research.

I hope I have conveyed here the richness contained within this book and the pleasure I have had in reading it. Every chapter can be read in its own right as an essay of substance on a clinical phenomenon and related psychoanalytic theory. Taken as whole, the book is an example of psychoanalytic clinical research enquiry and questioning at its very best.

BUT FACTS EXIST

La Théorie ç'est bon, mais ça n'empêche pas d'exister.

Charcot, quoted by Freud (1893f)

But facts are cheels that winna ding
An' downa be disputed:

from "A Dream" by Robert Burns

Introduction

This book consists of an enquiry into the psychoanalytic theories that have been constructed to explain the clinical observations that can be made in the course of the psychoanalytic investigative and therapeutic work with patients suffering from mental disorders. This enquiry begins (see Chapters 1 and 2) with Freud's theoretical expositions presented during the period between 1894 and 1917 (Freud, 1894a, 1900a, 1914c, 1915c, 1915d, 1915e, 1917d). It then turns to Freud's new theoretical stance (1920g, 1923b, 1926d) on the same clinical phenomena that had been the basis for his first theoretical formulations. These new theoretical perspectives (Freud, 1920g, 1923b, 1926d) have provided the foundations for the revisions of psychoanalytic theory and practice introduced by Klein, Fairbairn, the object relations school (Balint, Winnicott), and Kohut. The clinical phenomena that are characteristic of symptom neuroses, character abnormalities, psychoses, and organic mental states justify the appellation of objective clinical facts. They occur independently of any one specific observer and are "... verifiable through repeated similar observations" (Abrams, 1994). The symptoms and signs of mental

1

disorders meet these criteria. Symptoms issuing from the somatic manifestations of anxiety, compulsive thoughts, abnormal perception of a bodily part (dysmorphophobia), and delusional content are objective clinical facts. So are such signs of mental illness as compulsive acts, psychomotor retardation, active and passive negativism, and perseverative phenomena.

A different situation exists when it comes to the data that emerge during psychoanalytic treatments. These data arise within a special context—namely, the patient–analyst relationship. To emphasize this, they have been described as psychoanalytic clinical facts, in order to distinguish them from objective clinical facts. Psychoanalytic clinical facts, it is asserted, are the creation of the patient–analyst interaction (Orenstein & Orenstein, 1994; Reisenberg-Malcolm, 1994). For example, a patient fell silent during a session but responded to an interpretation designed to make him aware of a resistance against further disclosures. He said, somewhat reluctantly, that on his way to the analysis he had had the phantasy of rescuing the analyst from a fire that was consuming her house (a transference phantasy, Freud, 1910h). Another patient who was unable to reach his full intellectual and vocational potential provided "material" in which he supplanted his father and brother. His success in life meant their deaths. Psychoanalytic facts thus exist in the sphere of psychical reality (Caper, 1994; O'Shaughnessy, 1994). It is this that predominantly distinguishes them from clinical facts in that they are not verifiable outside the patient–analyst situation.

Another difficulty arises from the suspicion that psychoanalytic facts are not independent of the analyst's theoretical preferences (Orenstein & Orenstein, 1994; Sandler & Sandler, 1994). How are psychoanalytic facts to be disentangled from the analyst's interpretations? The hermeneutic interpretation of the psychoanalytic process has been a reaction to the problem of verification. According to the hermeneutic tradition (Habermas, 1971), psychoanalytic facts are aspects of a narrative produced in the analytic situation (Schafer, 1994; Steiner, 1995). The analyst is a novelist, not an archaeologist (Chertok & Stengers, 1992). The narrative can be interpreted, but its subject matter is of a different order from that data which is susceptible to the methods of natural science. In Ricoeur's (1977) opinion, there are no facts nor any observation of facts in psychoanalysis—there is only the interpretation of a narrated history.

The differences amongst analysts about psychoanalytic facts led Caper (1994) to write: "The psychoanalytic controversies between people who have different views about what constitutes a psychoanalytic fact may not be resolvable."

Frequently overlooked in discussions about clinical facts and psychoanalytic facts are phenomena that repeatedly appear in the course of psychoanalytic treatment and that fulfil criteria demanded for clinical facts. These phenomena are neither specific nor unique to the psychoanalytic situation. They may appear or have appeared in other inter-personal relationships. This is true for typical dreams (Freud, 1900a), as well as for dreams with a frustrating content. Apart from dreams there are the parapraxes that may make their way into a psychoanalytic treatment. Then there are the wish phantasies of adolescence and the masturbatory phantasies that owe nothing to the analysis as far as their origins are concerned. There is therefore a category of observations, clinical facts, that may appear in the course of an analysis, which are not the creation of the interchange between patient and analyst.

It is the recurring phenomena (clinical facts) whose existence is independent of a specific observer that provide the foundation for Freud's theory of the healthy and disturbed mind (1900a, 1915c, 1915d, 1915e, 1917d). The clinical examples described in Chapters 1 and 2 have been selected not to support Freud's theories but merely to demonstrate how his observations led to his explanatory concepts. This caveat obviates the criticism, frequently made and repeated recently by Spence (1994), that psychoanalysts are in the habit of presenting only those phenomena that appear to substantiate Freud's theories while leaving out those that do not.

The clinical facts described in this book are largely drawn from the author's experience of working as a general psychiatrist and as a practising psychoanalyst (Freeman, 1965, 1969, 1973, 1976, 1988; Freeman, Cameron, and McGhie, 1958). The range of clinical facts comprises the symptom and character neuroses, the functional psychoses (the schizophrenias and manic depressions), and organic mental states (acute and chronic brain syndrome). An excellent opportunity was afforded to observe how far psychoanalytic theories and therapeutic techniques are explanatory and therapeutically effective in mental disorders that rarely fall into the purview of the practising psychoanalyst. It may be said that the functional psychoses and organic mental states provide a testing ground for the value and validity of the psychoanalytic facts that emerge during the treatment of these conditions. The phenomena of these psychoses do not accommodate themselves to a purely clinical theory, as in the case of the symptom and character neuroses (see Chapter 9). For this reason, Freud's metapsychological concepts (see Chapter 1) require to be retained despite their abstract nature, which too easily suggests that they are somehow disconnected and apart from clinical observations (Holt, 1981).

Psychoanalysts and psychiatrists are deprived of the objective measures that enable physicians and surgeons to establish definitive diagnoses and evaluate responses to specific treatment measures. In view of this, it is incumbent upon psychoanalysts to record carefully clinical facts and their own reactions, and particularly to examine the history and foundations of the concepts they employ for the purpose of explanation and interpretation. It is to be hoped that this book will contribute positively to the many ongoing debates in the societies of the International Psychoanalytical Association—not least the issue of whether psychoanalysis belongs within the province of the natural sciences.

CHAPTER ONE

The clinical foundations of Freud's pleasure (unpleasure) principle

The theory of the pleasure principle is in essence an attempt to explain why wishing is ubiquitous in the lives both of the mentally healthy and those afflicted by mental pathology. Soon after Freud began to treat and investigate cases of hysteria and obsessional neurosis, he observed the close relationship that exists between the symptomatology and the wishes that were unacceptable to the patient (Freud, 1894a, 1896b). These wishes, which had once been conscious, had been automatically (involuntarily) dismissed from consciousness. This was because they had evoked anxiety and guilt. In the absence of satisfaction, these wishes found substitutes whereby they might become conscious. Patients' dreams fell into this category. Apart from dreams and neurotic symptoms, however, wishing and psychical wish-fulfilment, substitute formations, and the reactions they engender may be observed at first hand in those psychoses, at the onset or in chronicity, where there is extensive psychical dissolution.

I

In the case of dreams, wish-fulfilment is not immediately obvious. This is particularly so when the wish is obscured because it is unwelcome to the dreamer's consciousness. The fulfilment of wishes that is found by the analysis of dreams must be seen in the context of the way in which the latent dream thoughts find representation in the manifest content of dreams (Freud, 1900a). The following dream of a patient in psychoanalytic treatment is illustrative.

> This man dreamt that *his cat, of whom he was fond, had defaecated twice on the carpet. He was very angry and had the impulse to kick the cat out of the house.* The content of the dream was logical and at odds with the belief that dreams are incapable of reasoned thought. However, there was one discrepancy between what actually happened on the dream day and the dream content that requires explanation. On the dream day, the cat did soil the carpet, but only once, not twice. The patient said that he liked cats but found their inscrutable manner, self-sufficiency, and unreliability irritating. He immediately thought of a man whose assistance he had often to call upon in the course of his work. He distrusted him because sometimes he gave the impression of being deceitful. When the patient turned to "twice" in the dream, he recalled that on the dream day he had to cancel his analytic "hour". After doing so, he remembered that he would have to cancel a session later in the week. He was uneasy about this, fearing that he would be considered unreliable and not to be depended upon. He feared the analyst would "kick him out".

As is generally the case in the construction of dreams (Freud, 1900a), a parallel had been drawn between the patient and the cat on the one side and the patient and the analyst on the other. As will be seen, the logical content of the manifest dream belonged to the latent dream thoughts. In sleep the patient was concerned with the thought that although the cat was dependent on him, he was equally dependent on the analyst. He was dependent on two men neither of whom he was sure he could trust, but he needed their assistance. He feared the analyst's anger for being unreliable like the dirty cat. Only anger with the cat could find its way into the manifest dream content. What could not find its way into the manifest dream was his rejection of the criticism that he was unreliable and dirty. There was no means by which the dream thought—"No. I'm not afraid, I'm angry with you [the analyst]"— could be represented in the manifest dream. In this dream the relationship of similarity (to be the same as) that could not find verbal expression in the dream was achieved by identification. The patient was identified with the cat on the basis of their having in common the characteristics of unreliability and dependency. The analyst also substituted for the cat on the basis of his inscrutability and possible untrustworthiness. Cat/analyst and the man whose help he needed were identified with one another. The fear of the analyst's anger in the latent dream thoughts was reversed in the manifest dream with his becoming the one who was angry. Reversal was the means of expressing a contradiction in the dream thoughts. He contradicted the thought that he was afraid of the analyst's anger for being unreliable. The wish that things were the opposite was fulfilled by reversal. His wish to soil the analyst obtained a psychical reality—a psychoanalytic fact.

In this dream there was a plethora of substitutions—cat for patient, cat for analyst, and the other man. The cat represented the relationship between the patient, the analyst, and the other man on the basis of their possessing characteristics in common. Condensations of this kind and substitute formations in conjunction with wishes psychically fulfilled are the empirical data of dreams. Similar phenomena are also encountered in the thought disorder that is characteristic of the non-remitting schizophrenias of the hebephrenic–catatonic type. The utterances of these patients, consistently or periodically, do not conform to grammatical rules and thus appear as nonsensical as dreams often seem to be.

A long contact with these patients is necessary before their speech content can be understood.

Such a contact was possible with a man whose hebephrenic–catatonic schizophrenia had lasted uninterruptedly for many years. From time to time the word "masterpiece" appeared in his speech. It took a long time to put together the fulfilled wishes (delusion) represented by the single word. One day when angry with the author he shouted: "Don't dare to insult the masterpiece." The masterpiece was himself. As fragments of coherent and intelligible speech occurred, usually under the impact of some affect—anger, jealousy, sadness—it was possible to recognize that prior to the illness he had written a poem for a girl he believed loved him. He gave it to her, much to her amazement, saying: "I've written this for you, it is a masterpiece." He revealed that he greatly admired Salvador Dali's picture of the crucified Christ, which was in the local art gallery. A further understanding was gained when he said that he had been martyred three times and pointed to three scars on his wrist. He had been in three mental hospitals. One day he asked, "Do you know what thrice [ter] is in Latin?" Parts of the word "masterpiece" had their own meanings for him. Master represented his secret belief that he was the crucified Christ who had risen on the third [ter] day. As Christ, he had restored the hospital after its destruction (his variant of the "End of the World" delusion) and redeemed the patients and staff. He had brought peace (piece) to the world. His reward was reunion with his girlfriend.

As a result of the dissolution of the cognitive organization that underwrites logical thought, the patient could only express his psychically fulfilled wishes in the manner available to the healthy dreamer. Hence similarity could only be expressed through identification. In this way the masterpiece expressed the belief that he was as handsome as Salvador Dali's Christ. The different trains of thought (wishes fulfilled) were condensed into the substitute "masterpiece". He was Christ the Redeemer, he had been thrice martyred and brought back to life, he had saved the world and was reunited with his girlfriend. As a dream can only express "No" by reversal of its content, so this patient's wish delusion contradicted the reality of the actual situation in which he was a helpless victim.

II

These clinical vignettes demonstrate that the wishes that are embedded in dreams and in the thought disorders of long-standing cases of schizophrenia result from the need to relieve unpleasure. In the dream it was the unpleasure of hate and dependency. In the psychotic patient it was the unpleasure of longing. In the neuroses and the psychoses unpleasure from sexual frustration leads to wishing, but the expression of the psychically fulfilled wish is often interfered with and obscured by a censorship.

A woman with a neurosis had the following dream. *Her former husband was trying to force his way through her bedroom window.* She wakened in fear. On the night of the dream she had been making love with her man friend. He ejaculated prematurely, leaving her unsatisfied and restless (the unpleasure of frustration). The wish fulfilled (the attempt to relieve unpleasure) in the dream was having coitus with her potent husband. However, as such a conscious wish was unacceptable to her, she reacted with anxiety.

This transformation of sexual excitement into anxiety was also to be observed in the case of a married woman suffering from schizophrenia. She claimed that a former lover interrupted her sleep by standing outside her house, shouting sexual obscenities. He did this, she said, because he was sexually excited and angry because she ignored him. Here also the unpleasure arose from sexual excitement that could not be satisfied. Her husband was, actually, impotent.

Identification may be the means whereby a wish, psychically fulfilled and springing from longing, finds representation in both dreams and psychoses.

A woman school teacher who was in psychoanalytic treatment had the following dream. *She roughly shook a girl pupil and said in a sharp voice: "You will not ruin my class."* This kind of behaviour was foreign to the patient's character. She had never behaved this way with children. During the course of her associations to the dream she talked about a female colleague who had the reputation of being a disciplinarian. The patient believed that the headmaster approved of this colleague because she often found them talking together. The patient desperately wanted the headmaster's admiration and wished he would subscribe to her liberal approach to education. Through behaving in the dream as the female colleague, she fulfilled her wish to be close to the headmaster. The longing was dissipated. Behind the figure of the headmaster stood the analyst and father. The colleague was a substitute for her sister, of whom she was and had been jealous.

The representation of a psychically fulfilled wish by means of identification has a direct expression in schizophrenic psychoses.

A woman patient fell ill with a psychosis that followed a remitting and relapsing course. During an acute attack she accused her sister of being jealous of her. This came to a head when she was "baby-sitting" to allow her sister and brother-in-law to join an invited audience for a television show. During the evening she formed the conclusion that her sister had arranged a change of identities—she had become her sister, and her sister had become the patient. The sister had done this out of jealousy because she wanted to thwart the patient's wish to meet a distinguished actor at the TELEVISION show—an actor the patient (delusionally) believed loved her. The identification with the sister enabled the patient to achieve her wish to be in her sister's shoes and at the same time attribute the jealousy and envy to her.

III

The forms that dreams and psychotic phenomena assume lead in their own way to the theory of the pleasure principle. Dreams have the form of an hallucination experienced as an immediate event. These formal characteristics cannot be explained (Freud, 1900a) on the basis of displacement, condensation, and means of representation that transform the latent dream thoughts into the manifest content of a dream. In the case of the psychoses, phantasies, agreeable and disagreeable, are experienced as realities (delusions). Memories are revived as hallucinations or lead to the misinterpretation of perceptions. The stream of thought as expressed in speech is disturbed in different ways (blocking, switching), and its content is subject to derangement, as in the case described above. These formal characteristics cannot be explained on the basis of the mental conflicts that may be discerned within the content of the psychopathological phenomena. Thus hallucinations whose content is the voice of a lost beloved, as in a maniacal psychosis that follows real object loss, cannot be attributed solely to the loss itself or to the wish (fulfilled) to be re-united with the loved one.

Delusions are compelling experiences. They are often ephemeral, and in the case of the non-remitting schizophrenias the content changes in the course of the illness (Bleuler, 1911; Freud, 1911c). In the case of persecutory delusions, the persecutor may be known or unknown. Where the persecutor is unknown or is a phantasy figure, careful study of the patient over a period of time generally reveals that he/she is a substitute for someone with whom the patient had a close relationship in reality (parent, parent substitute, lover) or for a wished (phantasy) relationship. In long-standing cases of schizophrenia, the connection between un-pleasure and wish-fulfilment on the one hand and substitute formations on the other is most easily observed. In these cases the persecutory delusions of the onset recede, and with the exception of periodic but passing bouts of persecution, are replaced by wishful delusions, as in the "masterpiece" patient. The unpleasure of frustration and longing is attenuated by phantasies whose content is replete with substitute formations.

The theory of the pleasure principle

I

The theory of the pleasure principle is composed of concepts that are at the heart of Freud's (1900a) theory of mind as described in the seventh chapter of *The Interpretation of Dreams*. By turning to the history of the concepts their essential nature may be fully appreciated. Much misunderstanding has been caused by the failure to do this (Solms, 1996).

Prior to 1895, Freud and Breuer (1893a) were searching for a theory that would connect the symptoms and the affects observed in hysteria. To do so, they turned to familiar concepts—those belonging to the neurophysiology of their day. This neurophysiology postulated that the networks and chains of neurones that constitute the central nervous system were activated and inhibited in much the same way as an electrical system used for lighting and power (Breuer, 1895b). A certain level of tension must exist within the system so that any one part of the system may be activated when necessary. Similarly in the nervous system, an optimal level of excitation must be present at rest and so be prepared for work. Resistance between neuronal networks ensures that the functioning of a particular neuronal system would not be interfered with by the activity of another neuronal complex. Excitations were thus conceived as akin to pulses of electrical energy, varying in strength, which could pass to different neuronal networks as required. In modern neurophysiological terms excitations may be thought of as the action potentials that accompany the propagation of the nervous impulse along the axis cylinder of the neurone. If the levels of intracerebral excitation caused through exogenous and endogenous stimulation reach a critical level, then an outlet had to be found, preferably in motor action. The principal task of the nervous system was therefore to "... keep intracerebral excitation constant" (Breuer, 1895b). This theory, which Freud (1920g) was later to describe as the "Principle of Constancy", is in accord with the physiologist Claude Bernard's (1867) concept of "La Fixité du Milieu Interieur".

Breuer's (1895b) introduction to his theoretical chapter in *Studies on Hysteria* (Freud & Breuer, 1895d) reveals directly that his usage of neurophysiological concepts to explain mental events was a "second-best". Their usage was not to detract from the ideal of clothing theoretical ideas of abnormal mental events in "the language of psychology". He goes on: "If instead of an idea we choose to speak of excitation of the cortex the latter form would only have meaning for us in so far as we recognized an old friend under that cloak and tacitly reinstated the idea" (Breuer, 1895b).

Freud hypothesized (1894a) that a failure of affect expression was at the centre of symptom formation in hysteria and obsessional neurosis. What was the source of the affects? What determined their transformation into symptoms? Breuer (1895b) conceived affects as the conscious expression of excitatory processes. Affects being conscious were distinct from excitations. Affects ". . . go along with an increase of excitation" (Breuer, 1895b). Excitations occur outside consciousness. Apart from physiological needs and exogenous stimuli, the most important source of increases of excitation is the sexual instinct (Breuer, 1895b). In the mentally healthy, heightened intracerebral excitation, from whatever source, is reduced through discharge in the form of affects—anger, fear, sexual affect, and so on. If such discharge is obstructed, for whatever reason, the level of excitation remains high. Under these circumstances expression of affect is blocked, and the underlying excitatory processes find another form of outlet—as, for example, in their transformation into motor or sensory symptoms, as in conversion hysteria.

Freud (1900a) espoused Breuer's psychological theory of hysteria and went much further. He abandoned his attempts to formulate a neurophysiological theory of mind and instead decided to ". . . remain on psychological ground" (Freud, 1900a). The neurophysiological concepts—excitations, innervations, inhibition, resistances—were now given a purely psychological connotation (Solms, 1996).

To complete the "psychologizing" of his theory of mind, Freud (1900a) replaced the concept of excitations by the concept of cathexes. Like excitations, cathexes are the psychical representations of the demands that instinct makes upon the mind. They are without quality—that is, they are without ideational accompaniments. Alone they can never be known to consciousness (Solms, 1996). To become conscious, they must make connections with the memory traces of words and images. The ease with which substitutes are formed in dreams and in states of psychical dissolution suggested to Freud (1900a) that there is in these mental states no hindrance to the movement of cathexes from one memory trace to another. The cathexes must possess a mobile quality. Such a quality is absent in the thinking of the mentally healthy adult in the waking state. Otherwise purposive thought would be impossible.

The cathexes "energizing" this logical thinking must therefore have lost their mobility by becoming bound through a process of inhibition.

II

Freud's (1900a) theory of the nature of wishing is based on the clinical observations made on dreams and mental pathology (see above). A build-up of cathexes leads to unpleasure. This is most apparent when the occasion for unpleasure is a bodily (instinctual) need. Wishing is a reaction to unpleasure—that is to say, a wish consists of the revival of the experience of a past satisfaction in circumstances of the build-up of unpleasure. The psychical fulfilment of a wish in dreams and psychoses is thus the means whereby a build-up of cathexes may be avoided. This hypothesis follows in the footsteps of the early theory (Breuer, 1895b) that for the nervous system to work efficiently "intracerebral excitation" must be kept at a constant level. Wishing is then a function of the mind (mental apparatus, Freud, 1900a), which ensures that cathexes cannot pass beyond the range that guarantees its optimal functioning. Dreams, hallucinatory and delusional phenomena show that psychical wish-fulfilment cannot in itself bring about a completely satisfactory reduction of unpleasure. It is a movement in that direction. Pleasure is gained when the unpleasure is removed by satisfaction of the wish, in reality.

Freud's theory (1900a) that wishing first appears in infancy as an hallucination the (theory of hallucinatory gratification) rests, first, on the observations that dreams have an hallucinatory quality and, second, on the wishful misinterpretations and hallucinations that follow real object loss in maniacal states and schizophrenic psychoses. Freud (1900a) hypothesized that the infant, like the dreamer and the hallucinating patient, experiences unpleasure when there is a build-up of cathexes whose focus is the missing love object. In the case of the infant, unpleasure is indicated by crying and restlessness. This is assuaged when there is an experience of real satisfaction of the hunger. When hunger returns, there is once more a build-up of cathexes and resulting unpleasure. As hypothesized for the dream and hallucinatory phenomena, the cathexes causing the unpleasure revive the memory trace of the infant's last act of satisfaction. There is a revival of the memory but as an hallucination—that is, as an external perception. The unpleasure that has been created is momentarily abolished by the hallucinatory experience.

As the achievement of perceptual identity (i.e. memory and the hallucinated experience of satisfaction) does not have the same effect as real satisfaction in the case of the infant, the need continues. This psychical state brings about means, other than that of achieving perceptual identity, of ensuring the satisfaction of need. This requires the inhibition of the process whereby the cathexes find their way to the memory traces, causing them to be experienced as an hallucination. The cathectic process is terminated at the memory trace and does not proceed to perception. In the psychoses and organic mental states, the inhibitory process succumbs to the psychical dissolution with memories reappearing as hallucinations.

The inhibition imposed on the drives to find immediate relief of unpleasure has the effect of binding the mobile cathexes that are characteristic of the system Freud (1900a) designated the primary process. Immediate wish-fulfilment, through the reduction of unpleasure, is the sole aim of that psychical system. The inhibition of the movement (topographic regression) to perception (i.e. hallucination) is the function of a second psychical system (Freud, 1900a). This system, the secondary process, with its voluntary control of the musculature, capacity to differentiate, perceptual modalities, and access to memory schemata, binds and redirects the cathexes arising from need to the external world, where possibilities exist for achieving a real perception of the object from which satisfaction may be obtained. The second system is no less concerned with achieving the dissipation of unpleasure (i.e. the fulfilment of wishes), but it has at its command other means of obtaining this.

Freud's (1900a) theory, that a complex type of mentation (secondary process) emerges out of an undeveloped form of mental activity, reveals the impact that Darwinian evolutionary concepts had upon him. This influence had been present from the days of his studies on aphasia (Freud, 1891b). The immediate source of this influence had been Hughlings Jackson's (1884) theory of the evolution and dissolution of the nervous system (Stengel, 1953).

III

The phenomena of dreams and psychoses demonstrate that the psychical dissolution that takes place in these states of mind does not bring to an end the potential for unpleasure. Longing, object loss, and sexual need can, each in its own way, cause a build-up of cathexes (excitations, Freud, 1926d) and lead to unpleasure. The theory of the pleasure principle is explanatory in that it proposes that different phenomena follow from the pathway chosen by the mobile cathexes pursuant of their aim of "drive discharge", leading to a diminution of unpleasure (wish-fulfilment). In the case of dream hallucination and the hallucinations of psychoses, the cathexes, no longer bound as result of the partial or complete dissolution of the secondary process, follow a backward course (topographic regression, Freud, 1900a) within the mental apparatus to its perceptual end, where they revive auditory and visual memory traces of real events that return as perceptions. The disorder of logical, conceptual thought is a consequence of the cathexes reviving the mental representation of words and things in such a way as to lead to substitute formations and condensations.

Illustrative is the case of a 35-year-old divorced woman who had been ill with a non-remitting schizophrenia for over seven years. Her illness was characterized by persecutory and grandiose delusions. These had a sexual content and were in the nature of passivity experiences. Sexual sensations were constantly inflicted on her, she believed, by hospital staff and other unknown persons. She reluctantly agreed to meet the author to discuss her sense of victimization and her wish to leave the hospital. After a few meetings during which she talked about her delusional experiences, including her belief that she was a princess, she became silent, withdrawn, and sullen. She got up, and just as she left the room she shouted, "They are all dirty, Persian Oil and Glasgow Royal. Oil is mental." This "condensation product" was understandable because of information she had given to a nurse with whom she was periodically friendly and also from what was known of the history of the illness. This utterance contained within it memories of her un-happy life in Persia with her husband, where he worked with the oil company. He had been unfaithful to her, and now she was a prisoner in the mental hospital. "Oil is mental" gave expression to her conviction that it was her husband who was ill and not herself.

This woman, like the healthy dreamer (Freud, 1900a), could not give expression in her thinking to causal relationships and to such logical connections as "because", "and", "the same as" (similarity), or "no". She had lost the capacity to express in a grammatically correct form the thoughts that her husband had abandoned her because he had another woman. He was dirty—the same as the dirty oil with which he worked. He had deserted her because she was ill. She was imprisoned in a mental hospital (Glasgow Royal) by her husband and his accomplice the author, where she was subjected to sexual abuse—"They are all dirty, etc.".

Concomitant with these thoughts was the wish delusion that she was a princess, wrongfully treated. This reversal of her real situation (patient in a mental hospital), and indirectly conveyed in her angry outburst, was the way she expressed the wish that things were the opposite to the way they were. This was the only way she could say, "No, it's not true that I am ill and frustrated sexually. It is my husband who is insane and dirty." This rejection, as in a dream, was made possible by the elementary mode of mental operations brought to the fore by the psychical dissolution. It was this primitive thinking that facilitated the defence (I am not ill, my husband is, etc.). The aim remains the same—the reduction of unpleasure and its replacement by wish-fulfilment. Under the conditions of sleep and in the schizophrenias of the non-remitting type, the ego system *Pcpt–Cs*, already disengaged from reality, is now available for the reception of ideational complexes (phanta-sies, etc.) that have become the focus of mobile cathexes. As belief in reality is bound up with the senses, phantasies become delu-sions (see Chapter 9).

The pleasure principle is a psycho–biological, dynamic—economic theory having its base in the concept of the mental derivatives of instinct (cathexes). It is non-structural. The psychical representation of objects that are the focus of bound and unbound cathexes are afforded their due importance. The clinical examples illustrate this clearly. The pleasure principle is economic in the sense that it does not depend on a series of theoretical assumptions. It is founded on the concept of unconscious mental processes (cathexes) which are without quality until they find representation in the memory traces of percepts, things, and words. Further, when there is a build-up of mobile cathexes following the demands of instinct, outlets must be found in action, thought, and perception to maintain the effective functioning of the mental apparatus. When successful, this reduces unpleasure and leads to real or psychical wish-fulfilment.

The theory of the pleasure principle demonstrates that Freud judged the value of his theoretical formulations in accordance with their proximity to clinical observations. The introduction of the structural theory (see Chapter 4) did not lead him to diminish the importance of the hypothesis of the pleasure principle (Freud, 1940a). It was securely based on clinical phenomena and could not be brushed aside.

CHAPTER TWO

The theory of repression

Observations that neurotic patients are reluctant to speak freely about their real life and psychical experiences led Freud (1894a, 1896b) to postulate that an involuntary mental process opposed self-revelation. Therefore, from clinical work with patients suffering from hysterical and obsessional neuroses, the theoretical concept of repression was derived. The importance Freud attributed to the concept, as central to an explanatory psychopathology of the neuroses, is attested by the fact that he devoted a paper to the subject (1915d) and then returned to it in the paper on "The Unconscious" (Freud, 1915e).

The analytic treatment of the transference neuroses (hysterias, obsessional neuroses) had shown that an instinctual impulse, expressed mentally as a wish, and which should have led to pleasure had been replaced by anxiety. This occurred because of the impact of psychical influences inimical to the fulfilment of the particular wish. The clinical phenomena of the transference neuroses provided Freud (1915d) with the means of describing how repression operated. These "characteristics" of repression, as he called them (Freud, 1915d), are best illustrated by recourse to clinical observations.

A man aged 34 suddenly developed a marked tremor of his right hand while having a meal with his mother in a restaurant. He feared he was having a stroke. A further attack occurred within a few weeks. Soon fear of the tremor occurring stopped him from using a knife with which to eat or writing with a pen in the company of others. This avoidance (phobia) increased its power over the succeeding months, leaving him virtually confined to the house. At this time he sought analytic treatment.

The analysis revealed quite quickly that the immediate cause for the onset of the neurosis (an anxiety hysteria) was taking another man's wife as a lover. The night before the attack of tremor in the restaurant, he had coitus with her for the first time. It later transpired that he had had a similar but transient attack, although less severe, in late adolescence. This took place when his eldest brother brought his fiancée home for the first time. When he saw her he simultaneously experienced genital arousal and his right hand shook. A similar experience occurred during the analysis. While staying in a hotel, he found himself in a lift with a young bride leaving her reception to go back to her room. As he looked at her his hand began to shake and he felt anxious. The onset of the neurosis was accompanied by a loss of sexual desire and partial impotence. Afterwards he could only "conjure up" sexual excitement by phantasizing secret sexual adventures.

After a period of analysis a most important determinant of the choice of symptom came to light. In late boyhood and adolescence he phantasied being a great magician. He became adept at conjuring tricks carried out with his right hand. He performed his tricks for family and friends and obtained much pleasure from their applause. He remembered that in earlier days he had the phantasy of being a fox. Foxes lay low, watched for their chances, and struck when unexpected. In his masturbatory phantasies he waited for his opportunity to entrap a woman and then treated her as ruthlessly as the fox his victim. A variant of the fox (masturbatory) phantasy was disclosed later and was again significant for the choice of symptom (the tremor). He phantasied spinning a web, like a spider with which to catch a woman.

As the analysis developed, a plethora of material emerged comprising feminine identifications (mother and woman friend) and phantasies with passive, sexual aims: "How nice to be a woman and be looked after." He imagined himself as a woman lying on her back with her legs apart waiting to be penetrated. At this time he was aware of a heightened anal erotogeneity. He phantasied penetrating himself anally with a penis-like object. He was playing the parts of man and woman in coitus. This had its repercussions in the transference. At the beginning of the analysis he feared being criticized for his sexual behaviour. Later and contemporaneously with the passive–feminine sexual phantasies, dreams revealed his fear of being deceived, tricked, trapped, and ill used by the analyst. The analyst was now the fox who was about to treat him as he wished to treat the woman (a psychoanalytic fact). Thus the transference reactions gave expression to the resolution of his identifications with the woman in coitus with the man.

From a descriptive standpoint, the onset of the neurosis was characterized by tremor, anxiety, and the loss of genital sexuality. The unconscious psychopathological events that led to the complex of symptoms may be hypothesized as follows. Initially a preconscious conflict arose between forbidden heterosexual wishes and the fear of the real and psychical consequences of the fulfilment of these wishes. The result was that active sexual aims (sadistic and scoptophilic) were given up in favour of passive sexual aims (masochistic and exhibitionistic). Heterosexual object choice gave way to identification with the female love object. Anal erotogeneity made its appearance. The emergence of the passive (anal-femininity) led to a new, but completely unconscious, conflict between the wish to be a woman and the fear of losing his masculinity. The tremor was a compromise formation. It gave expression to his exciting sadistic sexual wish phantasies and it simultaneously symbolized the punishment for them—that is, becoming a woman. The model for this was his mother who had always suffered from a shaky hand.

The above example illustrates the connection that exists in the transference neuroses between the clinical phenomena and repression (Freud, 1915d). The tremor and the loss of active (genital) sexual aims showed that repression had acted to remove specific mental content from consciousness. The patient was no longer conscious of what had been a compelling sexual desire for his woman friend. There was anxiety instead. The analysis revealed that pleasurable sexual aims still existed in the "unconscious" but altered (active to passive) and directed to homosexual objects. Repression had led to substitute formations. The patient's anxiety was not abolished by the physical symptom of tremor as occurs in a typical case of conversion hysteria. In this case, as in others of anxiety hysteria, it was the concurrence of anxiety and the loss of the ideational content of the heterosexual wishes that led Freud (1915d) to hypothesize that these losses occur because repression acts differentially on the complex of ideas and the "quota of affect", which together comprise the instinctual representation.

Repression leads to the removal of the ideas and acts against the affect (the quantitative factor) by converting it into anxiety. Clinical phenomena of the kind described above led Freud to propose that change of affect is by far the most important result of repression in the anxiety hysterias—"If repression does not succeed in preventing feelings of unpleasure or anxiety from arising, we may say that it has failed, even though it may have achieved its purpose as far as the ideational portion is concerned" (Freud, 1915d). As will be described in Chapter 5, Freud (1926d) later reformulated his ideas about the relationship between anxiety and repression.

In Freud's papers (1915c, 1915e), which take a theoretical perspective on repression, this process is conceived as one that consists of a withdrawal of ("energic") cathexes from the ideational component of a wish phantasy with the removal of the affect or a change in its nature. If repression only acted by the withdrawal of cathexes from ideas, it would have to be constantly repeated to ensure the unwelcome ideational and affective complex was kept permanently from consciousness. For this to happen, a counterforce was essential—a countercathexis (Freud, 1915d) that could exert continuous pressure on the proscribed ideas.

The analysis of the transference neuroses had revealed that the content of the symptom often had its source in phantasies (Freud, 1916–17). In the case of anxiety hysteria described above, masturbatory excitement connected with phantasies of the "omnipotent" hand had a passing conscious expression in late childhood and adolescence. Later they were subject to repression. Cathexes had been withdrawn from the wish phantasy. With the aid of a counter-cathexis they remained preconscious until the advent of the analysis and their return to consciousness. Freud (1915d, 1915e) argued that preconscious phantasies of this kind, which had been conscious at some time, had forerunners that had never been conscious at any time. He distinguished therefore between mental events (wishes etc.), which once had conscious expression and were then repressed, and those events that had never found their way into consciousness (primal repression).

Primal repression

Freud (1915d, 1915e, 1918b) was led to the concept of primary repression by acknowledging that to understand the genesis and specific features of certain symptoms, phantasies, and behaviour, these phenomena must be the expression of early childhood experiences, the memory traces of which never achieved consciousness. His clinical experience led him to conclude—"Such memory traces, then, have nothing to do with the fact of becoming conscious; indeed they are often most powerful and most enduring when the process which left them behind was one which never entered consciousness" (Freud, 1920g).

Quite apart from other approaches (dreams, screen memories, etc.) the content of masturbatory phantasies described by patients is often of such a specific nature as to indicate, that their source must lie in sexual experiences of early childhood which could never be remembered because they were never conscious. The following is illustrative.

The patient, an unmarried man of 27 years of age, entered analysis because of depression of mood and loss of interest in life and work. He was despondent and self-critical. At work he found himself staring vacantly in front of him while time slipped by. He had great difficulty wakening in the morning, despite two alarm clocks and the radio. The somnolence, which often persisted into the day, gave rise to the suspicion of narcolepsy. He was investigated neurologically, but no evidence of organic disease was found. He became so despairing that suicidal thoughts were frequently in his mind. Treatment with antidepressant medications and electroshock therapy brought no improvement in his mental state.

He said that when he wakened in the morning his intention of the previous night to get out of bed immediately was always forgotten. After looking at the clock, he concluded that he was in good time and could stay in bed a little longer. When this period was up he felt there was no real need to hurry. When he eventually acknowledged that he was already too late to be in time for work he decided to stay in bed. He might as well be "hanged for a sheep as a lamb". Later he reproached himself for being idle and lazy.

As the analysis on a five-times-a-week basis was scheduled for the morning, he had great difficulty in arriving on time. He overslept, and this continued into the fourth year of the analysis. The depressive symptoms did not interfere with his capacity to participate in the analysis. He was friendly and not without warmth. Both mother and father transferences made a spontaneous appearance after a short time. The former was a constant source of resistance, not least in the sphere of sexuality. Illustrative was a transference dream in which *he masturbates and leaves the tissue with which he cleaned up in the bed. Mother would find it much to his shame and annoyance.* This dream led to his disclosing how difficult it was for him to reveal his sexual phantasies. His identification with his mother, who had suffered from a depressive illness for as long as he could remember, resolved into its component object relationships in the transference. This enabled his ambivalence to his mother, caused by disappointments at her hands and her restrictive attitudes, to have full emotional expression. The transference from the father was a source of difficulty because of guilt. His fears for the author's health and state of mind mirrored deep concern for his father who had always been helpful and supporting. In childhood his father had assumed the mother's role when she was in a depressed state. Gradually he was able to recognize that, for him, success in life must lead to his father's psychical death. This, in conjunction with the analysis of the identification with his depressed mother, led to the disappearance of the depressive symptoms.

In the year or so before puberty he constructed a phantasy of an extendible breast. The material for this sexual phantasy, be believed, was based on a visit to the zoo. He had been excited and fascinated by the way the elephants used their trunks to eat and drink. In the phantasy a breast-like structure issued from an aperture in the female genital region. It had a multi-purpose function. It could grasp solid objects, suck up liquids and gases and could even be used to assist locomotion.

In adolescence the breast phantasy disappeared and was replaced by others with a similar scoptophilic aim. Common to these adolescent masturbatory phantasies was the image of a woman inserting and then withdrawing objects from her vagina. The objects were cylindrical in shape. The phantasy ended with his examining the vulva to ensure that the objects were wholly within. With some difficulty he disclosed that in adolescence he phantasied being about to rape his young sister but desisting at the last moment. Despite this he is a ruined man. In another phantasy he is accused of rape and charged in court. He knows that he is innocent and can prove it. He allows the case to proceed and undergoes interrogation by the prosecutor. Then he confounds him with his evidence and is honourably discharged. In reality this young man was shy and awkward in the company of women. He disapproved of sexual promiscuity unless there was the intention of marrying.

A dream led to his remembering a detail of his earliest conscious sexual phantasy. In this dream *he is looking at his penis. He is leaning back on a table or desk and a man is trying to have coitus with him face to face.* On the dream day he phantasied having coitus with a girl who worked in his office. In the masturbatory phantasy she is leaning back, half clothed, against a desk. He then recalled that in a childhood phantasy of a wedding, the bridesmaids were leaning back on a table similarly unclothed. This identification with the woman, revealed in the dream, was repeated in a further series of dreams in which, as in the one described, he played the parts of both man and woman in coitus.

In the fourth year of the treatment dreams occurred, while asleep in the morning, which became accessible to analysis. There was much resistance to their recall. The first dream was reported ten minutes before the end of the session. Its symbolic content pointed to a primal scene phantasy—*A boat was being pushed up an inclined ramp. The aerial on the boat was bent. There were soldiers wearing helmets and men whose hair was cut in the fashion of a tonsure. His father was in the background.* Had he actually seen his parents or others during and after coitus? Had he seen a condom—the helmet? Had he seen a deflated penis—the bent aerial? Was the penis he observed circumcised—the tonsure? At this time the patient was encouraged to follow his thoughts and report his dreams without interventions on the author's part. He reported later that his father was partially circumcised.

Two days after the dream he related another morning dream which portrayed his identification with the (sexual) father. In this dream *he is wearing a pair of trousers and a jacket that belonged to different suits. He is riding a horse with a woman and he is attempting coitus with her.* He recalled an occasion when his father had appeared at breakfast wearing trousers belonging to another suit. Next day he brought a dream that suggested that the repressed memory of the parents in coitus was only able to find expression via the transference—"He feels himself to be a woman. A man behind him is trying to have coitus with him but then he becomes the man himself." Here he is the woman (mother) with the author (father). Then in identification with the author he is the man (father) having coitus with the woman (mother)—a psychoanalytic fact.

In the next session he returned to his phantasies of inserting and withdrawing cylindrical objects from a woman's vagina.

He disclosed that on several occasions he had attempted to insert a slim pencil into his urethra. This behaviour represented once more the act of coitus, with his playing the parts of man and woman. It was in the course of working on another morning dream that he suddenly had the visual image of a blood-stained Tampax (a menstrual tampon). The patient's dream had led to thoughts about a woman at work. He had observed that she was absent regularly every month for about two or three days. It was at this point that he had the image of the stained Tampax. He was taken aback because he had never actually seen a Tampax, certainly not one with clotted blood on it.

It was put to him that his morning dreams were actually memories of early childhood visual experiences (Freud, 1918b). These events had a mental registration but had never been conscious: hence his inability to remember them. Sleeping in the same room as his parents, he was awakened early in the morning by the noise of their coital movements. When they realized that he was awake and filled with curiosity, he was admonished and told to go back to sleep. Nevertheless he had observed the insertion and withdrawal of the penis. Such an observation was possible because the coitus had occurred outside the bed, with the woman leaning back against it and the man standing (cf. the masturbatory phantasy). In adult life it was a matter of "deferred obedience". He awakened and then went back to sleep.

The visual image of the blood-stained Tampax permitted another reconstruction which could be envisaged as intimately connected with the primal scene experience. His masturbatory phantasy in which he had to ensure that the cylindrical object was fully inserted into the women's vagina suggested that he had seen his mother remove a used Tampax, discard it, and carefully insert a new one. This is not a fanciful idea, because it is not uncommon for mothers to take young children into the bathroom with them if there is no one with whom to leave the child. As both erect penis and the Tampax are cylindrical in shape he had confused the one with the other. In his masturbatory phantasies he was both his father inserting the penis/ Tampax and his mother removing the penis/Tampax.

Within a matter of days after the reconstructions the patient began to waken spontaneously, without the aid of the alarm clock. Rather than being oppressed by a sense of hopelessness about the forthcoming day, as was usually the case, he had a feeling of optimism. He got out of bed immediately instead of going to sleep again. This spontaneous awakening continued for several weeks. Then the old feeling that there was no need to hurry began to get the upper hand, and he would fall asleep again. Then he had a dream, the analysis of which led to a sustained recovery of the ability to waken in the morning and get out of bed. In this dream *his trousers were disarranged, and he was trying to hide a condom.* He had been reading a humorous novel in which condoms figured prominently. Rather than consider the dream as relating to a transference anxiety, it was interpreted as a memory of his father trying to prevent him from seeing a condom. The next morning he awakened spontaneously. The working over of this material the next year led to the virtual disappearance of the somnolence.

What has been described thus far and what is to follow indicates that real events in the patient's early childhood had provided the stimulus for phantasies that had both an exciting and defensive aim. There was excitement connected with the phantasy of the extendible breast. This enabled him to deny the perception of the fact that his mother did not have a penis. The penis was hidden inside but when necessary could appear and be seen.

The analysis of his castration anxiety began with a dream. This occurred many months before he had the image of the Tampax covered with clotted blood. In this dream *he is in a tunnel, earth is falling on his head, and blood is trickling onto his face.* Before falling asleep on the night of the dream, he had been reading a book about the Vietnam War. There were vivid descriptions of the fighting that went on in tunnels constructed by the Vietnamese. The anxiety he felt in the dream was similar to that he experienced at the idea of being trapped in an underground place or buried alive.

No more was heard of this anxiety for some months, until one day he remembered his mother telling him about intercourse, pregnancy, and childbirth. He was about eleven or twelve years of age at the time. While recounting this memory, he suddenly had a visual image of a worm-like creature with teeth moving about in a cavern with slime on the floor and walls. The image alarmed him.

The phantasy of being trapped and injured in a tunnel or underground space was countered by the masturbatory phantasies of inserting and withdrawing cylindrical objects from a woman's vagina. In the former phantasy his trapped body stood for his penis in imminent danger of being caught and damaged. In the latter phantasies the ease with which he could remove the cylindrical object was a reassurance that he could save his penis from injury. Witnessing the removal of the Tampax provided him with a realistic basis for this defensive (wishful) masturbatory phantasy. Inserting the cylindrical object in phantasy or in reality into his urethra gave expression to his identification with the menstruating woman (reference the dream in which blood trickles onto his face) inserting the Tampax/penis. Through this defensive identification he could reassure himself that women did have a penis. The phantasy of the distensible breast was an elaboration of this.

The clinical data in this case favours in every respect the hypothesis that what the patient observed in his early childhood was registered mentally but did not become conscious. This was not simply because he did not have the words that would have enabled him to become aware of what he had seen or that reflective awareness was not sufficiently developed. More significantly, from the standpoint of the theory of primal repression, looking had led to a build-up of unpleasure with the drive to relieve this through satisfaction of the scoptophilia. However, the actual sight of the mother's genitalia and the blood interfered with this process. Descriptively, excitement turned into anxiety. Repression here did not consist of a withdrawal of cathexis from word representations, because they did not exist. This must be what Freud (1915d) meant when he wrote, "When it comes to describing primal repression, the mechanism just described of the withdrawal of preconscious cathexis would fail to meet the case: for here we are dealing with an unconscious idea which as yet has received no cathexis from the preconscious and therefore cannot have that cathexis withdrawn from it." Primal repression is a once-and-for-all process brought about by the imposition of a counterforce (an anticathexis) on the psychical events engendered by instinctual arousal. The scoptophilic content of this patient's masturbatory phantasies of later childhood and adolescence indicates that they were derived from the observed events that succumbed to primary repression. These latter phantasies were subject to repression, by virtue of cathexes being withdrawn from their ideational representations.

Both the patient who suffered from anxiety hysteria and the patient just referred to remembered their masturbatory phantasies of later childhood and adolescence. Neither had any recollection of real or psychical experiences in early childhood that determined the content of these phantasies. This is a commonplace observation in the psychoanalytic treatment of symptom and character neuroses. When patients recollect experiences of the recent or distant past, they usually claim that they had not discovered something new. They had always remembered the particular event or mental experience. These are the observational data. Freud's theory of repression offers an explanation of the two kinds of amnesia—one penetrable, the other only penetrable by way of reconstruction.

CHAPTER THREE

Freud's theory of mind reformulated: *Beyond the Pleasure Principle*

In *Beyond the Pleasure Principle* (Freud, 1920g) reformulates his earlier (1900a) theory of mind. The concept of the pleasure principle is the hub of that theory. The empirical data on which it was based are wish-fulfilment and the reactions that it evokes. As detailed in Chapter 1, wish-fulfilment is defined (Freud, 1900a) as a mental process resulting from a build-up of cathexes *pari passu* with instinctual arousal. The reduction of this build-up leads to unpleasure being replaced by pleasure. The channels of motility, affect, and thought are employed to bring about the reduction of the unpleasure. An inhibition is placed on this process with the cathexes being bound in the secondary process. The analysis of anxiety dreams and anxiety hysteria reveals that the unpleasure created by the psychical representations of instinct (cathexes) is not necessarily relieved and finds expression as anxiety. The pleasure principle is still operative but the potential for pleasure has been blocked by repression. It is a matter of pleasure in one system (unconscious) and unpleasure in another (conscious) (Freud, 1920g).

I

The traumatic neuroses, common in the 1914–18 war, led Freud to recognize that the pleasure principle could be rendered ineffective and no longer guide the direction of mental life. In the acute stage traumatic neuroses present with disturbances affecting the central nervous and autonomic nervous systems—tremors, fits, paralyses, disorders of sensation, vomiting, diarrhoea, disturbances of consciousness (stupor, amnesia). Once the neurosis has passed into a chronic stage there are repetitive dreams the content of which portrays the actual traumatic event. There are objective and subjective signs of anxiety, fatigue, exhaustion, and a sensitivity to noise. Patients with these symptoms do not, in the waking state, give thought to the traumatic event. This only occurs in dreams. If the pleasure principle were still in operation and dreams expressed wishes fulfilled, then these patients would, as Freud (1920g) points out, dream of recovery or dream of the period when they were healthy rather than suffer memories of the traumatic event.

Relevant here is Solms' report (1997) that a few of his patients suffering from aphasia said that their speech was normal when dreaming. The poet Milton, who became totally blind in 1652, wrote in 1658, in the sonnet "Methought I saw . . .", of a dream of his wife:

> "Her face was vail'd, yet to my fancied sight,
> Love, sweetness, goodness, in her person shin'd
> So clear, as in no face with more delight.
> But O as to embrace me she enclin'd
> I wak'd, she fled, and day brought back my night."

The pleasure principle (wishes fulfilled) remained in the ascendancy.

Until the traumatic neuroses became the object of study the hypothesis of a build-up of unpleasure within the mental apparatus was attributed to the demand the derivatives of instinct (cathexes) made upon the mind (Freud, 1920g). The traumatic neuroses showed that unpleasure will result when the mental apparatus is flooded by external stimuli. The traumatic event has the effect of rupturing the shield that protects the mental apparatus from excessive external stimulation (Freud, 1920g). This leads to a disorganization of the secondary process (loss of control of motility, etc.) and to the loss of its inhibitory function (failure of repression). Unbound cathexes come to dominate mental life and find expression in the symptoms of the acute stage of the illness (tremor, fits, etc.). As repression is no longer effective in containing the unpleasure generated by the unbound cathexes, other means have to be found to achieve this. Freud (1920g) suggested that the repetitive dreams, the inability to concentrate, the exhaustion followed from attempts to bind the mobile cathexes, restore the secondary process and the protective shield of the mental apparatus. To bring this about—"An anti-cathexis on a grand scale is set up, for whose benefit all the psychical systems are impoverished, so that the remaining psychical functions are extensively paralysed or reduced" (Freud, 1920g).

Traumatic dreams gradually disappear when the traumatic event and the associated affect is abreacted. This suggests that when unpleasure is relieved the secondary process is re-established. Repression can now act to inhibit unpleasure once again. When this happens, the pleasure principle asserts itself, and dreams regain their function of wish-fulfilment. The following clinical example describes the sequence of clinical events.

A man of 30 who had served in the Navy during the 1939–45 war had been in a ship that was torpedoed. He spent some hours in the water before being rescued. After this event he began to suffer from insomnia that had special characteristics. This continued for several years after his discharge from the Navy. After going to bed he would immediately fall asleep, being fatigued, but then he would waken in a short time. He would then fall asleep and waken again. This cycle of events continued through the night. A psychotherapeutic treatment helped him to remember that when he went back to sea after being torpedoed, he was fearful of falling asleep lest the ship be attacked and sunk. Thus he would lie down fully dressed. In spite of his fear, fatigue triumphed and he fell asleep. He would waken with a start in a few minutes. This sequence of waking and sleeping would continue until morning. His insomnia improved considerably after these recollections. Here the repetitive waking up can be interpreted as the expression of attempts directed at avoiding the unpleasure of the memory of the traumatic event.

II

That patients in analysis repeat in the present thoughts, affects, and behaviour which have their source in the past is one of Freud's early discoveries. The analyst's task is to bring these repressed unconscious contents into memory while allowing the patient full expression of them in the present. Fundamental for the viability and success of the analysis is the patient's ability to recognize that he is reliving a forgotten past. Often what is repeated, Freud (1920g) observed, is of a distressing nature. This did not necessarily contradict the pleasure principle, because pleasurable wishes may bring anxiety in their wake leading to resistances of different kinds. However, clinical experience had shown that there are repetitive phenomena that cannot be considered as arising from wishes that had once afforded pleasure and had subsequently been repressed. These latter repetitive manifestations, whether appearing as transferences or in real life outside analysis, could never have been a source of pleasure. Like the repetitive dreams of traumatic neuroses, these phenomena occurring in the course of analysis indicate that the pleasure principle had been rendered inoperative by the compulsion to repeat.

The following instance illustrates in some detail how childhood experience, real and psychical, may lead to unpleasure which it is beyond the pleasure principle to regulate. This case is of special interest because the patient, a married woman 40 years of age, had a recurrent dream that turned out to be the result of a traumatic event that occurred when she was about 30 years old.

This patient came to analysis complaining of depression of mood, loss of self-confidence, tremulousness, palpitations, sensation of choking, and pain over the right temple. Treatment by tranquillizers and hypnotics had led to a dependency on them. However, she was able to stop taking the tranquillizers soon after the analysis began. Her marriage was an unhappy one.

This patient came regularly and on time to the analysis. She was responsive to the request that she reveal everything that came to mind. At first she talked of her unhappiness with her husband and the sense of responsibility that she felt towards her mother. At home she complied with her husband's every wish, in many respects behaving like a valet-cum-maid-servant. She was careful to say things to him that he would find acceptable and avoid anything that might annoy him. Her behaviour with her mother was similar.

When she began to complain about her symptoms and the efforts she was making to come to the analysis without much appreciation on the author's part, it was possible to point out to her that she felt the same way about her husband and mother. Analyst, mother, and husband were equated. This led her to remembering that in adolescence it was her responsibility to look after her mother, who was frequently depressed and took to her bed. When the depressive mood passed her mother behaved as if nothing had happened, never thanking her for her efforts. On one occasion she was so angry she threw a knife at the door. Today, as then, she had to stifle her anger for fear of her husband's displeasure.

The transference was well established as was shown by her reaction to the first holiday break. Her symptoms were worse, the author was unsympathetic and indifferent. He was as demanding as her mother. These criticisms were not easily expressed because she feared the author would get fed up with her. She would be left without anyone to help her. She hated this thought but admitted that she had feared that the author would die during the holiday, and she would be left alone. The expression of these transference thoughts was followed by dreams that revealed the extent to which she had been traumatized in childhood.

In the first dream of the series *the patient's daughter was angrily accusing her of taking too many hypnotic pills.* This had happened in fact. However, the dream reminded her of frightening nights with her mother when her father was away from home, as he often was, for long periods. She now knew that her mother's distressed and confused state at night and in the mornings was the result of her addiction to barbiturate hypnotics. In the middle of the night the patient would be wakened by her mother's moans and screams. She would go to the mother's bedroom and the door would be locked. The patient would return to her bed and lie in fear. She remembered asking her mother not to take the barbiturates. These memories were followed by an anxiety dream in which *she is being attacked by a brown dog. She runs to the room where her husband is sleeping, but the door is locked, and he will not open it.* She wakened in terror. Further memories revealed that this anxiety dream belonged to another complex of traumatic events—namely, violent rows between the parents.

The dream that led to these memories was one in which *she was trying to prevent her mother from falling. The mother's reaction was to shout at her. Her mother's eyes were piercing and full of hate.* On the dream day she was telephoned by a woman who has the same colour of eyes as her mother. Some years previously the woman had accused the patient, unjustly, of having an affair with her husband. This caused the patient to recall that for as long as she could remember her father had had a mistress— one reason for his many absences from home. The patient was witness to furious rows between the parents. These rows wakened her in the night. In later childhood she would try to intervene on her mother's part. She was terrified by the physical violence that often occurred. *The brown dog* of the previous dream reminded her of the fact that her father had a suit of that colour. In that dream she was identified with her attacked mother.

In early childhood the patient had a closeness with a nurse-maid, who gave her the love and affection that was missing in the relationship with her depressed mother. The nurse suddenly left and the patient could not understand why. She was devastated by this event. This relationship found a repetition as a transference alongside that of the mother. Like the mother, the author was critical, unresponsive, and demanding; like the nurse, he was a protector. She often looked upon the analytic session as a refuge from life at home with her husband (mother). In a dream *she is with the author, happy and secure. Then her husband appears and dismisses the author. She is distraught, clings to the author's legs, but he is dragged away from her.* She wakened in terror. This dream was followed by others in which a similar sequence of events occurred—happy then frightened. Breaks in the analysis led to fears of abandonment. It was this fear that had, in the past as well as in the present, made her acquiescent and compliant. It was only after her resistances had been dissipated that repressed traumatic events of her childhood could find expression, indicating that the compulsion to repeat must be attributed to the "repressed unconscious" (Freud, 1920g).

As mentioned above, this woman reported a recurrent dream. In the dream *she is swimming. Then something hits her on the right side of the head. She is gasping for air and choking.* She would waken in fright. On the occasion when she first reported the dream, she had no associations whatsoever. Later she was able, with some difficulty, to remember the incident to which the dream gave representation. She and her husband had been boating on a lake. They had taken a lunch basket and drinks. They had quarrelled, she had fallen overboard, and she had accidentally struck her right temple on the side of the boat. Dazed, her head had slipped beneath the water. She had tried to swim but her legs had become entangled in some weeds. Her mouth had filled with water and she had been unable to breathe. Fortunately her husband had managed to grasp her and pull her out of the water. Her symptoms of choking and pain in the right temple were memories of the traumatic event.

Striking instances of the pleasure principle being overruled by the compulsive repetition of frightening and painful experiences are to be found in schizophrenic psychoses. In those cases that follow a non-remitting course it is not uncommon to observe, despite medication, patients who abuse themselves verbally and physically while referring to themselves in the third person.

An unmarried woman 36 years of age had been ill for 16 years. At the onset of the psychosis she complained that an unknown man was taunting her, commenting on her thoughts and actions and tempting her to acts of promiscuity. During the chronic stage of the illness she was withdrawn, inattentive, and negativistic. Periodically there were acute attacks during which the following repetitive behaviour appeared. These were usually associated with a change in her usual routine. The episode to be reported took place when she was being seen daily in an attempt to initiate a therapeutic relationship. Her speech content consisted of threats, commands, and warnings. The threats were expressed in a fury of rage—"I'm going to hit you", "I'll have no mercy on you" (slapping herself). As to commands—"Keep your tongue between your teeth", "Never appear here again". Then the warnings—"You mustn't dare to do these things." After striking herself, she shouted—"I had to hit her, she is a bad girl." These utterances were repeated for half an hour, and then she reverted to a withdrawn, inaccessible state. She clearly resented being intruded upon, and her threatening attitude demonstrated this.

What events were being dramatized here? They were clearly of a traumatic nature. There are schizophrenic patients in whom the origin of the repetitive self-punitive behaviour can be easily identified.

An unmarried woman 26 years of age fell ill a year after her father's death, when she was 20 years old. She said that her brother, also unmarried, whose bedroom was next to hers, was putting thoughts into her head while she was asleep. He had come into her room in the night and, unbeknown to her, had raped her. During the chronic stage of the illness she believed that others were using her tongue to speak thoughts that were not her own (transitivism). Unlike the patient described above, she was willing to talk about herself. After four weeks of daily meetings a change took place. She was silent, and it was only with encouragement that she spoke. She said that she had gone for a walk with a male patient the evening before. He had kissed her. At this point she reported that a voice was saying, "How's about a kiss?" and her lips formed a kiss-like movement. Then she struck herself violently upon the head. "Why did you do that?" she was asked. She replied that a voice in her head had said, "You're not too old to be hit." She remembered that her father would say this. He was in the habit of striking her if she disobeyed him.

A comparison between the traumatized neurotic patient described here and the schizophrenic patients reveals one significant difference. In the former the repetition, as transferences, of the traumatic events of childhood only came to light after the resolution of resistances. This reflected their repressed status. In the case of the schizophrenic patients, the repetitive behaviour occurred immediately or within days of starting daily meetings. Was this immediacy of response to meeting with the author caused by the absence of resistance? Such an absence could be attributed to the lack of repression attendant on the psychical dissolution present in cases of non-remitting schizophrenia. If Freud's theory of traumatic dreams is followed, then a similarity may be discerned between the repetitive dreams of traumatic neuroses and the schizophrenic phenomena referred to here. In the former the protective shield of the mental apparatus has been damaged, allowing the ingress of stimuli which lead to the build-up of unpleasure. In the instance of the schizophrenic patients the repression barrier is no longer effective. This allows the intrusion of stimuli from within the mental apparatus, again leading to unpleasure. In both categories, it may be hypothesized, the compulsion to repeat reduces the degree of unpleasure by binding the stimuli from within and without. A similar hypothesis is applicable to traumatic events of childhood. These lead to unpleasure as a result of the mental apparatus being flooded by stimuli. The compulsion to repeat acts to reduce the unpleasure.

III

The compulsion to repeat can replace the pleasure principle, in the presence of psychopathological events. This led Freud (1920g) to conclude that the compulsion to repeat was of a more elementary nature than the pleasure principle. The action of the compulsion to repeat suggested ". . . something more primitive, more elementary, more instinctual than the pleasure principle which it overrides" (Freud, 1920g). With the appearance of the secondary process the compulsion to repeat gives way to the pleasure principle as the determinant of the course of mental events. The build-up of unpleasure in the mental apparatus is inhibited (repressed) and no longer has free access to the second system (preconscious), thus ensuring the integrity of the functions of that system.

Freud's assertion that the compulsion to repeat had all the qualities of an instinct required a revision of his theory of instincts. Freud's (1916–17) first theory of instincts derived from his work with the transference neuroses. He postulated a dualistic (biological) theory based on the observable conflict between the sexual instincts and the ego instincts. Included within the ego instincts was the function of self-preservation (the self-preservative instinct). The psychological ego (the self) had the potential for aggression in the service of that aim quite apart from its functions as a repressing, censoring, and critical agency. A modification of this theory became necessary in the light of phenomena that required for their explanation the hypothesis of a transposition of libido (sexual instincts) between self and objects (introversion of the libido in the neuroses; withdrawal of libido in the psychoses). An original ego libido had to be postulated (Freud, 1914c). This narcissism is the libidinal component of egoism (Freud, 1914c). That the ego instincts possessed a libidinal component rendered the dichotomy of sexual instincts and ego instincts untenable. A libidinal component was integral to the instinct of self-preservation.

Freud's (1920g) concept of a death instinct followed from his perception of the repetition compulsion as instinctual in nature. Like the repetitive nature of the character of instinct in animals, clinical and other data suggested that the repetition compulsion led to the revival of pre-existing mental states. In Freud's (1920g) view there was ". . . an urge inherent in organic life to restore an earlier state of things" (Freud, 1920g). The conservatism had to coexist with "creative" trends arising spontaneously within the organism or caused by the impact of external events. This led to organic development. However, these "advances" were deceptive. Whatever changes occurred, the nature of the instincts was such as to ensure that a silent and continuous pressure was exerted to bring about their annulment by restoring the original nature of things. The logical conclusion to the argument (Freud, 1920g) was that the aim of instinctual life is to lead to death—to a return to the inanimate.

The theory that the aim of the death instinct is to bring about the end of the organism's life did not sit easily with an instinct of self-preservation. This contradiction was resolved by Freud (1920g) by ascribing to the self-preservative instinct the task of ensuring that the path of the drive to death was not interfered with or prematurely ended by circumstances beyond those whose purpose was the death of the individual—"What we are left with is that the organism wishes to die in its own fashion. Thus the guardians of life, too, were originally the myrmidons of death" (Freud, 1920g). As the sexual instincts alone stand in opposition to the death instinct, they transcend the death of the individual through the coalescence of the germ cells and the creation of a new organism. The sexual instincts are therefore the true life instincts (Freud, 1920g).

The theory of the life and death instincts now posed a question the answer to which was to have momentous consequences for Freud's thinking and for future psychoanalytic theorizing. How could the sadistic component of the sexual instincts be an integral element of the life instincts when the aim of the sadistic impulse was to inflict injury on the object? Freud's (1920g) answer was that sadism must be an expression of the death instinct, which under the influence of narcissistic libido was forced away from the ego (self) and directed to the object. Masochism could be thought of as a primary expression of the death instinct and not, as previously held, the consequence of sadism turned upon the self (Freud, 1915c).

Freud (1920g) speculated further that the direction followed by the sexual instincts—the sexual organizations and the component instincts—would be determined by the sadism that had been extruded from the ego. The death instinct, via sadism, thus entered into the service of sexuality. Instinctual development could be regarded as a process in which there was a merging of libido and sadism (life and death instincts). It is this admixture that imprints the drive and momentum to each stage of sexual development. Thus in the genital organization of the libido, for example, sadism provides the libido with the power to possess the love object for

the purpose of coitus. The intensity of ambivalence that characterizes an individual's relationships to his love object is determined
by the extent to which sadism has been attenuated by libido. With
the introduction of the theory of the life and death instincts, Freud
(1920g) revised his belief that instincts can neither love nor hate
(Freud, 1915c). Love was now a derivative of the life instincts:
hatred a derivative of the death instincts turned from the self and
directed to objects. Unpleasure caused by external objects, as in the
earlier theory, was no longer considered to be a precursor of hate.
Thus there was no need in looking for an explanation of hatred to
revert to the concept of a self-preservative (ego) instinct that hated
and wished to destroy external objects causing unpleasure.

The pleasure principle (Freud, 1900a) also succumbed to the
theory of the life and death instincts. The processes leading to the
reduction of the level of "excitation"—unconscious mental processes (see Chapter 2)—within the mental apparatus are removed
from the ambit of the pleasure principle and allocated to the death
instinct. A new concept, the Nirvana principle, is postulated,
whose action is to convert "The Restlessness of Life . . . into the
stability of the inorganic state" (Freud, 1920g). The Nirvana principle is put on the same footing as the pleasure principle, whose
operation is limited to the impact of the life instinct (libido) on the
mental apparatus. By attributing the movement to reduce unpleasure to the death instinct, the theory of wishing based on the
pleasure principle (unpleasure to pleasure) was no longer sustain-
able. Wish-fulfilment, real and psychical, proceeds under the
governance of the Nirvana principle.

IV

Beyond the Pleasure Principle thus marks the reformulation of the
1900a theory of mind—a reformulation based on new theoretical
ideas and explanatory concepts. With sadism removed from sexuality and attributed to the death instinct, aggression and destructiveness were afforded a significance that was absent when they
were believed to belong to the ego instincts.

Freud's (1920g) reflections on his theory of the life and death
instincts shows that he found it difficult to throw aside his belief

that theory should not stray too far from clinical observations. Was he doing just that by wandering into biology to find support for the theory of the death instincts? The theory did not have the sound empirical base of the theory of the sexual and ego instincts, which are amended to take account of narcissistic libido. He writes (Freud, 1920g)—"It is true that my assertions of the regressive character of instincts also rests upon observed material—namely on the facts of the compulsion to repeat. It may be, however, that I have overestimated their significance." Towards the end of *Beyond the Pleasure Principle* he admits he is not sure if he believes in it himself.

Freud's (1920g) open-mindedness invites a closer examination of the repetition compulsion in all its manifestations. Is it necessary to invoke a death instinct to account for it? May there not be another explanation for the repetition compulsion that does not diminish its significance as a fundamental characteristic of mental life?

The compulsion to repeat has its most direct and impressive expression in the repetitive dreams of the traumatic neuroses. Here it is not necessary to infer that transference thoughts and affects are repetitions of traumatic childhood experiences. The dreams of traumatic neuroses faithfully reproduce the traumatic event. The event was the necessary condition for the appearance of the neurosis. The part that predisposition plays in traumatic neuroses is difficult to determine or assess. Conjecture only arises retrospectively. It is of interest to speculate whether the patient who fell into the water and was nearly drowned would have dreamt of her life-threatening experience if she had been mentally healthy. Traumatic neuroses occur in individuals who were mentally healthy prior to the trauma. This is most strikingly observed in those individuals who only succumb to a traumatic neurosis after they have been repeatedly subject to life threatening experiences. In these individuals, usually soldiers in action, no evidence is forthcoming of a "neurotic constitution". This suggests that a predisposition, acquired or constitutional, is not necessarily a precondition for the emergence of a traumatic neurosis as it is in a transference neurosis.

If real events are capable of evoking the compulsion to repeat, *de novo*, as in the traumatic neuroses, it would seem logical to

assume that the mainspring of the powerful and painful transference repetitions found in the analysis of symptom and character
neuroses must be real (traumatic) events of childhood. Freud
(1933a) wrote later—"Transference neuroses are here offering an
extreme case; but we must admit that childhood experiences, too,
are of a traumatic nature." In the following excerpt from the analysis of a young unmarried man transference phenomena occurred
that fulfilled the criteria of being beyond the pleasure principle. In
this case, were real events alone responsible or had phantasy
played a major role in imparting a traumatic quality to commonplace childhood experiences?

The patient aged 26, suffered from bouts of derealization and
depersonalization that caused great anxiety. In an attack he lost
his sense of identity and his surroundings appeared unreal and
unfamiliar. As to the former, he said: "I could be anyone." He
felt lost in a real sense, and even if found, he would be uniden-
tifiable. He had no memory of ever having been lost in childhood. He recalled his mother telling him that she had been lost,
and how frightened she had been. His symptoms limited his
life in the most serious way. He was afraid to walk alone in the
street or take public transport. Essential journeys were made
by car where he felt relatively safe, but even here attacks could
occur. He had discovered that he could keep fear at a distance
if he had the phantasy of being a particularly successful, so-
cially distinguished individual, but this was not uniformly
achieved.

For the first weeks of the analysis he was too frightened to lie
on the couch lest his symptoms occurred. He said that he felt
vulnerable lying down in the presence of another person.
Frightening ideas of being stabbed or strangled flashed
through his mind. He got round these fears by repeating to
himself that the author was a reputable medical man. He was
eventually able to lie down. For the first 18 months he was
most co-operative. He talked freely and provided much information about his life. His father had died suddenly when he
was 11 years of age. His mother suffered, and always had, from
"bad nerves". She had panic attacks and was agoraphobic. She

was extremely volatile and given to outbursts of uncontrollable rage. In such states she would lock herself in her room. This behaviour had terrified the patient when he was a child. Now he found her to be intrusive, and he resented this. Until the age of three and a half he had a full-time nanny with whom he remained when his parents went away. She was, he recalled, a disciplinarian, and he was afraid of her.

The atmosphere of the analysis changed after the initial 18 months. He began to doubt the analyst's integrity and on this account was reluctant to reveal his thoughts. He felt that interpretations were thrust down his throat without any right on his side to disagree. He wanted to arrive at his own conclusions and not have them made for him. Anyhow, the author was only trying to show how clever he was. When the author tried to get him to recognize the importance of following the rule of free association, he (the patient) accused him of being unhelpful and intransigent. The analysis was destroying his self-confidence.

Accompanying these criticisms was the perception of the author as sinister and sadistic. The analytic room appeared dilapidated and run-down. He phantasied he might be hypnotized, unbeknown to himself, and misused in some way. When these thoughts entered his mind, he had to sit up or get off the couch. It would take some time before he could compose himself and lie down again. He revealed that these criticisms and frightening phantasies had been present for months, and his co-operative manner had been motivated by the need to keep the author "sweet" lest the author "go mad" like his mother. He recalled that in the early months of the analysis he had been uneasy using the lavatory lest the author lock him in the cloakroom and keep him prisoner. These phantasies and misperceptions had a near-delusional quality requiring, on his part, a great effort of will to acknowledge their unreality.

These transference phenomena were understandable in the light of what he had said about his relationship with his mother. In identification with her he criticized and verbally abused the author, as she had done to him. She criticized him for being deceitful, stubborn, conceited, and uncooperative. He had to appease her in case she lost her temper. He remembered her shouting and screaming at him. When she locked herself in her room he would cry outside the door, pleading with her to come out.

A further contributant to his childhood fears and repeated as transferences consisted of the relationship with the nanny. She had ceased living with the family in his fourth year but continued to come to the house during his childhood. The content of his fears about the author's malevolent intentions suggested that he had been subject to much bodily interference—forcible feeding (reference the protest that interpretations were thrust down his throat), the forcible administration of medicines, suppositories for constipation, and so on. His fear of being locked in the cloakroom by the author suggested that this had been a means of punishing him. In later childhood his mother would threaten to send him off to the nanny's house when he misbehaved. This threat never failed to terrify him. He remembered being in the nanny's house. She lived in a poor district, and the house was drab and dilapidated. This description of the nanny's house accorded closely with his perception of the analytic room. Equally significant was the fact that the content of his depersonalization symptom consisted of his being irretrievably lost in a poor, broken-down part of the town, which he was unable to identify. That the nanny was a threatening figure was evidenced by a dream he remembered having after his father died. In the dream *the nanny had died.* Rather the nanny than father—the wish for her removal was fulfilled.

Are transference repetitions that override the pleasure principle to be attributed to real events of childhood or to frightening phantasies that alter the way in which these events were experienced? It is well known that fear of assuming the recumbent position for analysis is commonplace in individuals who have in childhood been subject to seduction or to surgical and dental procedures. These events induce a sense of helplessness and vulnerability. It hardly seems possible in the present case that the patient's extreme behaviour—sitting up, jumping off the couch, and transient faults in reality testing—may be explained on the basis of phantasy alone. To do so would be equivalent to maintaining that the symptoms of a traumatic neurosis are caused by frightening phantasies.

The hypothesis that traumatic events in childhood provide a nucleus for the accretion of the content of phantasies is applicable in this case. The content of the patient's masturbatory phantasies suggested that sadistic impulses had taken the place of the passive sexual aims that had been enhanced by the traumatic experiences. In the phantasy he pictured himself as a strong, thickset man (quite the opposite to his own rather slender physique) who treated servants and women in a harsh and domineering manner. His perception of the author as a sadist was a projection of this sexual phantasy, which in its turn concealed masochistic sexual aims.

There is thus much support, then, for the hypothesis that real traumatic events in childhood act as stimuli rendering the pleasure principle inoperative. In this case, as in others of a similar kind, the regressive trend facilitated by the analysis led to a return of the repressed and with it the compulsion to repeat, the aim of which was to bind the mobile cathexes and to strengthen the secondary process.

V

Is there an explanation for the origin of the compulsion to repeat that does not depend on a theory of the death instinct? An alternative explanation is suggested by a phenomenon that occurs in cases of brain damage caused by trauma, disease (Alzheimer's disease, arteriosclerotic dementia, epilepsy, etc.), and in mental handicap. A repetitive tendency is a striking manifestation of these organic states. This tendency follows the psychical dissolution of the ego (secondary process). The extent to which the repetitive behaviour overshadows the operation of all mental functions—the fact that it bears no relationship to repressed mental contents—suggests that the pathological process has exposed a fundamental property of mental life.

These repetitive behaviours, subsumed under the concept of perseveration, occur in speech, in writing, in motor and sensory functions (Critchley, 1953; Schilder, 1953). In mental handicap perseveration shows itself in stereotypies and rigid patterns of behaviour. Goldstein (1943) and Luria (1965) have identified two distinct forms of perseveration. The first consists of the repetition of an action that ceases only when a new stimulus is presented to the patient. This form occurs in the non-remitting schizophrenias of the hebephrenic–catatonic type (Freeman & Gathercole, 1966), thus accounting for repetitive motor acts and stereotyped movements. The second form of perseveration comprises an inability to abandon a reaction to a stimulus when a new one is presented. The former has been called by Luria (1965) "compulsive repetition", the latter "impairment of switching".

When brain-damaged patients and the mentally handicapped are asked to introduce a new element into an accustomed activity, they become anxious, confused, bad-tempered, or withdrawn. This is to be observed when brain-damaged patients are undergoing a neurological examination that requires the patient to respond to a series of different instructions or when they are participating in psychological tests that involve speech and actions. The patient continues with one action when he should be responding to the next instruction. The affective disturbances which occur have been described as "catastrophic reactions" (Goldstein, 1943). Here the mental pain which has been evoked by failure to react correctly does not inhibit the repetitive act and bring it to an end.

Perseverative phenomena reveal in an exaggerated fashion the influence that preceding impressions (mental registrations) may have in the absence of an adequately functioning mobile attention. In brain-damaged patients there is ample evidence of a serious disturbance of consciousness and selective attention. The memory deficits (loss of vocabularies and short-term memory), confabulations and misidentifications attest to this. It is possible to hypothesize that in "impairment of switching" a causal factor is damage to the function of mobile (selective) attention. Attention becomes tied to the first mental registration(s) and is not available for new stimuli. This is not the case with "compulsive repetition". Here the introduction of a new stimulus brings the repetitive speech or movement to an end. Patients cannot voluntarily terminate a motor act. This is reminiscent of young children who are not able to end a voluntary movement at will (Luria, 1965). Dissolution of nervous functioning in the brain-damaged leads to an analogous phenomenon. The inhibiting mechanism that is yet to develop in the child is lost in the patient with chronic brain disease.

Repetition occurs over the whole range of mental functions. Pleasurable and disagreeable experiences repeat themselves psychically or in reality. There is repetition in the fields of cognition and motility. The phenomena that indicate that the pleasure principle is no longer in full command (i.e. dreams of the traumatic neuroses and disagreeable transferences) are repetitions of situations in which unpleasure from external events or internal circumstances cannot be dispelled. It is possible to hypothesize that these phenomena are caused by an "impairment of switching" no different from that which occurs at the sensorimotor level of mental functioning. The only difference is the greater complexity of the psychical organization of the former when compared with the latter. As long as the pleasure principle is in the ascendancy, although modified in its expression by the secondary process, the compulsion to repeat is subject to inhibition. This inhibitory influence is lost when the secondary process is weakened, as in traumatic dreams and in disagreeable transferences. It is important to recall (Freud, 1920g) that these transference repetitions make an appearance in an analysis after the resistances that oppose their expression are weakened—that is, when the secondary process is no longer in absolute control. In organic mental illness and in the non-remitting schizophrenias the inhibition is completely lost.

According to this hypothesis, the compulsion to repeat need not be thought of as having its origin in an instinct whose ultimate aim is to return life to the inanimate (the death instinct). Instead, it can be thought of as the expression of a constitutionally determined, innate property of mental life whose influence reaches through all levels. The degree of impact that this influence will exert on thought and behaviour will depend on how far the inhibition of its expression, imposed by the secondary process, is subject to impairment.

VI

Before concluding this chapter, it is worth referring to clinical phenomena, other than the compulsion to repeat, that must have led
Freud (1920g) to his theory of the death instinct. The self in a
variety of conditions (anorexia nervosa, dysmorphophobia, schizophrenic and manic-depressive psychoses) is no longer valued or
cared for. It is loathed and hated. Destructive attacks may be made
on physical or mental aspects of the self. In terms of Freud's
theory, this hatred and destructiveness is the expression of that
quota of the death instinct remaining in the self unbound by libido
(the life instinct).

The shift of hate and destructiveness from the self to others and
vice versa as well as the change from undervaluation to overvaluation is to be seen in the psychoses. The case of the schizophrenic
patient whose delusional reality was described in Chapter 1 is
illustrative.

The patient's illness began with fears of physical disease—tu-
berculosis and heart disease. He then complained that an unpleasant smell was emanating from his body. This disgusted
him. He feared going out because men were winking at him in
the street, suggesting that he was a homosexual. He made several serious suicidal attempts. Despite treatment, the course of
the illness over the next six years was to a "moderately severe
end state" (Bleuler, 1978). He was generally withdrawn, neglectful of his appearance and body, negativistic, and catatonic.

He was seen daily over a period of two years. Unlike the female schizophrenic patient described earlier in this chapter, he
was willing to join the author in daily meetings. He always had
to be sought out and never appeared of his own accord. Most of
the time he would ignore the author. A favourite habit of his
was to examine his face in the mirror of the interview room.
His negativism had both negative and positive aspects. As to
the former, he would ignore simple requests. An example of
the latter was the following. When greeted, "Good morning,
Mr Y," he would reply, "It is not good morning, Mr Y." His
relationship with the author never reached beyond a "need-
satisfying" level. His interest was confined to the wish that

the author would arrange for his irrational expectations to be fulfilled (i.e. be reunited with his phantasy girl friend; get a pension for life). While these delusional wishes were at their height, there was an accompanying overvaluation of the self— "I am a perfect art gallery face", he would say.

It was in the second year of the meetings that bouts of rage, which had occasionally appeared, became the order of the day. These rages occurred if he thought he was being contradicted or not properly understood. They were followed by a period of withdrawal, negativism, and catalepsy. He had lost patience with the author for not meeting his demands. He became increasingly threatening and domineering. Accompanying this was a change in the way he perceived himself. He found fault with his face. He blamed the author, other patients, and the television for causing this. Eventually he refused to attend any other meetings.

The clinical facts in this case may be interpreted in terms of Freud's (1920g) theory of the life and death instincts. A defusion of the libido (the life instinct) and the death instinct coincided with the psychical dissolution at the onset of the psychosis. Hatred and destructiveness were now free within the self, which was now regarded as repugnant and worthy of hate. There was no sense of guilt. The negativism and catalepsy that followed the suicidal attempts gave expression (were in a sense a defence) to the hatred that could not find overt expression. Later, under the conditions of the contact with the unsatisfying author, the hatred derived from the death instinct found an outlet.

Of particular interest in the context of the theory of the life and death instincts is the fact that when the psychosis was well established, the patient overvalued his body and in particular his face. It was as if the libido torn apart from the destructiveness of the death instinct could now be freely expressed. This occurred concomitant with the wish delusions. It was as if the patient was only capable of loving or hating his body. There was a lack of balance, it may be hypothesized, due to the defusion of the life and death instincts, with each pursuing its own aims independently of the other. Rosenfeld's (1971) concept of a destructive narcissism (see Chapter

8)—an overvalued capacity of the self as destructive—is derived from this formulation of the action of the death instinct.

There is an alternative explanation for the hatred and destructiveness directed against the self and others. This dispenses with the need to postulate a death instinct. It is an explanation founded on Freud's (1915c) earlier theory of the origins of hate. Hatred was then envisaged by Freud (1915c) as a reaction of the self-preservative aspects of the ego instincts (Freud, 1916–17) to unpleasure (see Chapter 1). On the basis of this theory, the rage expressed by the male patient and the female schizophrenic patient resulted from the unpleasure of disappointment at the hands of the author in the case of the former and the unpleasure evoked by the author's presence in the case of the latter. Hatred and physical attacks on others are then the result of the ego instincts striving to reduce unpleasure stimulated by contact with real persons. Destructive assaults on the body are, paradoxically, a desperate attempt by the ego instincts to preserve the mental self. Only by destroying the body can the unpleasure caused by bodily needs (sexuality), affects, and violent urges be removed.

Freud's (1920g, 1923b) admission that his theory of the death instinct was not based on new clinical observations casts doubt on the value of his decision to separate hatred and the potential for destructiveness from the self-preservative functions of the ego instincts.

CHAPTER FOUR

The new schema
of the mental apparatus
and its antecedents

Freud's (1923b) new schema of the mental apparatus did not result from the recognition of hitherto unexplained or unknown clinical phenomena. What was already known was to be approached from a new angle. It was in Freud's (1933a) words ". . . a question of new ways of looking at things and of new ways of arranging them rather than of new discoveries". Apart from the need to distinguish the unconscious ego from the repressed unconscious and account for the unconscious sense of guilt, there was the matter of the composition of the ego and the critical agency within the ego. It is important to recall here that Freud, prior to 1923 and occasionally afterwards, used the term ego to designate the self in its subjective and objective aspects. The clinical phenomena with which Freud was involved had been the content of the "Schreber case" (1911c), "On Narcissism" (1914c), "Instincts and Their Vicissitudes" (1915c), "Mourning and Melancholia" (1917e), and *Group Psychology and the Analysis of the Ego* (1921c). In what is described below it is easy to discern that the composition of the (structural) concepts of the ego and superego is based on the processes of identification that clinical phenomena so clearly portray. With the publication of *The Ego and the Id* (1923b), ego-object interactions (object relations) began to emerge at the centre of the psychoanalytic stage.

In constructing the theory of the ego and the id, Freud followed the principle that the phenomena of mental pathology are exaggerations of processes that, at best, can only be faintly observed in the mentally healthy—". . . we are familiar with the notion that pathology, by making things larger and coarser, can draw our attention to normal conditions which would otherwise have escaped us" (Freud, 1933a). The theories of the pleasure principle and repression, as determinants of healthy mental life, are based on clinical facts (see Chapters 1 and 2). Chapter 4 has the same purpose. A series of clinical phenomena, drawn from cases of neurosis and psychosis, are described to illustrate the pathological exaggeration of unconscious mental events that Freud discerned and which he used as the basis for the structural theory.

Antecedents of the new schema

I

In the Schreber case (1911c), Freud drew attention to Schreber's belief that his persecutor (Flechsig) experienced the same thoughts, intentions, and affects as he did himself. Freud (1911c) wrote ". . . [Schreber] expresses his firm conviction that the physician who influenced him had the same visions and received the same disclosures upon supernatural things as himself". Here Schreber did not distinguish his mental experiences from those of Flechsig as an object, although he retained his sense of identity. The clinical phenomena attendant on the onset of many cases of schizophrenic psychoses, similar to those of Schreber, suggest the following explanation for the retention of the sense of identity. These initial manifestations consist of transitivistic phenomena (Bleuler, 1911) that occur in the bodily and mental spheres. These—transitivistic— phenomena comprise perceptions of aspects of the self in the object and perceptions of aspects of the object in the self. There is uncertainty about the sense of identity. The transitivism may be understood as resulting from psychical dissolution. The almost immediate or delayed return of the sense of identity can be explained as the result of the restoration of an object relationship, albeit pathological, and psychical reconstruction (Freud, 1911c). It may be hypothesized that those aspects of the persecutor that were confused with the self (the transitivism) remain lodged within the self, leading to the patient experiencing himself as tied to the persecutor's intentions, sensations, and affects. The boundary between self and object has been restored, but at a price. Mental pathology thus exposes two forms of a relationship with an object—two forms of identification. There is one where the self and object are merged (transitivism) with a loss of the sense of identity, as in acute psychoses and organic mental states, and one in which there is identification with aspects of the object, but the sense of identity is retained. The psychoses thus provide empirical data for Freud's concepts of primary and secondary identification (Freud, 1921c).

Freud (1911c) hypothesized that unconscious homosexuality is instrumental in leading to other types of paranoia—delusional jealousy (delusion of infidelity) and erotomania. It is important to make the distinction between the concept of unconscious homosexuality and manifest homosexuality. Unconscious homosexuality describes the man's unconscious wish to play the part of a woman in coitus with a man. It also describes the woman's unconscious wish to act the man with a woman (Freud, 1911c; Frosch, 1983).

In delusional jealousy both the object and the self are perceived in a different manner than before the illness. Women afflicted by delusional jealousy hate their husbands and in this respect differ from instances of "healthy" jealousy, where the female rival is hated. Similarly, men hate their wives rather than the male rival. In cases of delusional jealousy the patients cannot turn their minds to thoughts that might throw light on their mental state. Working transferences do not develop. In some cases the delusional jealousy is replaced by a persecutory symptom complex (Freeman, 1990).

Intense and destructive jealousy is sometimes encountered during the analysis of women suffering from symptom and character neuroses. Information about the sources of this jealousy may

provide an explanation for the persecutory delusions that follow a
bout of delusional jealousy.

A married woman aged 33 began analysis complaining of depression of mood and bouts of derealization. Soon it became
evident that she was constantly suspicious of her husband's
fidelity without good reason. There were frequent outbursts of
jealous rage if she and her husband were in the company of a
woman the patient thought attractive. She switched off the
television if a pretty woman appeared on the screen. She was
convinced that thoughts of other women were constantly in her
husband's mind. She was vaginally anaesthetic and thus never
satisfied in coitus. She masturbated clitorally with exhibitionistic and sadistic phantasies in which she excited a man to erec-
tion, by his looking at her wholly or partially undressed, and
then frustrating him by denying coitus. When she agreed to
have coitus with her husband he had to fulfil certain conditions
in order to excite her. He had to tell her details of real or
imagined sexual encounters with women, despite the fact that
ordinarily such an idea would evoke rage. After intercourse
she would disparage him by scorning his potency and sometimes accusing him of being a homosexual.

As the analysis proceeded, she came to realize that she found
the women whom she accused her husband of being attracted
to, attractive to herself. She envied their physical attributes.
The jealous rages against the husband for his supposed infi-
delities led her to indulge in passing affairs with men in order
to revenge herself on him. She revealed that she hated having
to speak about occasions when she failed to capture a man's
sexual interest. This made her feel worthless. When she felt
that one or more men were competing for her attention, her
self-esteem was heightened. It was only with the greatest difficulty that she refrained from boasting to her husband about her
conquests. She had to admit that she obtained a similar pleasure telling the author about her affairs. The excitement was
similar to the excitement she felt when, at her request, she
got her husband to speak about his supposed sexual exploits
with other women. It was not difficult to get her to recognize

that she wanted to make a man (husband, author) excited and jealous.

This woman's sexuality was phallic with exhibitionistic aims. Her ego had been altered by a masculine identification (father, in the first instance). This masculine mode of relating continued throughout life and was expressed in her relationship with her husband and the author as a transference (psychoanalytic fact). Husband and author became the woman with whom she wished to act as a man—this quite apart from their representing the men she wished to be (narcissistic objects). Her morbid jealousy resulted from the externalization of her unconscious phallic masculinity and the need for a homosexual object.

The information gained from such an analysis gives some clues about the possible unconscious causes of the transition from delusional jealousy to a persecutory symptom complex. In the case just described the jealousy could be connected with unconscious exhibitionistic wish phantasies. The belief that they are being looked at and talked about in a critical way is a frequent complaint of female psychotic patients who previously believed that their husbands were unfaithful. These women conclude that the ideas of reference occur because others know of their husband's infidelity. The husband has confided details of their sexual experiences to his lover, and she has told everyone about it. This delusion is the counterpart to the excitement the neurotic patient obtained from describing her sexual exploits. It is possible to suggest that the psychotic patient unconsciously wishes to boast about her conquests but can only deal with this wish by externalizing it on to the persecutor.

The hypothesis that unconscious homosexuality lies at the root of erotomania finds support from two quarters. The first is from female patients who, in psychoanalytic treatment, develop an eroticized transference (transference love). The second is from a persecutory symptom complex following erotomania. In the case of neurotic patients who develop an eroticized transference, the heterosexual transference object has a forerunner in an adolescent homosexual object choice of a narcissistic kind (Freeman, 1984). The homosexual love object represented the self as wished to be. These patients exhibit a masculine orientation of the libido. Sexual excitement and satisfaction is confined to the clitoris. When these individuals achieved heterosexuality in late adolescence or early adulthood, the male object choice was a substitute for the earlier homosexual choice and similarly had a narcissistic basis. The second support for the homosexual theory comes from those female patients whose erotomania is succeeded not by persecution by the former beloved, but by a woman. The patient continues to believe in the constancy of her beloved but a woman, known to her previously, is obstructing with every possible means her reunion with her lover. Prior to the illness the patient had a positive, admiring attitude towards this woman. The female persecutor represented wished-for aspects of the self—a narcissistic love object.

In forming his theory of how the ego comes to be constituted, Freud (1923b) must have been influenced by the delusional content of the kind described above. This content illustrates how aspects of the mental and physical self are externalized onto objects and aspects of the object assimilated into the self. An alteration of the self follows along the lines of an identification with a former real or phantasy love object. Freud (1923b) proposed that the ego develops in this way. Its substance consisted of identifications based on previous object choices.

II

Papers published in 1910 and 1914 show that Freud (1910c, 1914c) was concerned with self–object relationships. Analytic work with male homosexuals demonstrated their pervasive identification with both the mother and the love object. The ego had been altered accordingly.

A homosexual man in analytic treatment had slept in his mother's bed until he was 4 years old. His father was rarely at home because of his work as a seaman. The patient recalled that his mother tended his body, bit him playfully, and caressed his buttocks. She was in the habit of cleaning his prepuce and to do so often had to restrict his movements. A brother was born when he was 4 years old, bringing the physical intimacy with his mother to an end. As a result of her attentions to his penis he masturbated excessively. His mother threatened him with the likelihood that his penis would fall off if he did not stop.

This patient's masturbatory phantasies gave expression to the bodily experiences with the mother. The patient's preferred phantasy was showing his penis to a boy, preferably immobilized, and masturbating him. A necessary condition was that the boy was not circumcised. Needless to say, the patient was not circumcised. In this phantasy the patient played the parts of mother and himself. A dream showed that he remained fearful of castration. In the dream *a boy is standing on a hillock. He holds a bird in his hand. He is very fond of it and strokes it. Then he releases the bird and it flies high into the air. He lifts a gun and shoots it. He is afraid of being found out and hides the bird under his coat.* In association to the dream he said that if he saw an attractive boy in the street, he would have an urge to exhibit his penis to the boy. He would take his penis out but hide it under his raincoat. The boy who excited him unconsciously represented himself and his penis. The dream had followed masturbation.

III

Analytic work with patients suffering from symptom and character disorders as well as those suffering from psychoses confirms Freud's (1915d) observation that the sexual instinct may be subject to a variety of vicissitudes other than repression. These changes in the instinctual derivative (sexual wishes) take place within the context of ego(self)–object relationships. It is this aspect of the matter that is relevant to the present discussion. Freud (1915c) singled out two vicissitudes to which the sexual instinct may be subject—a reversal into the opposite and turning round upon the subject's self. Reversal comprises a change in the aim of the instinct from active to passive and a reversal of its content. Turning round upon the self requires a change of subject while the aim of the instinct remains the same. To illustrate the processes at work, Freud (1915c) made use of the two pairs of opposites—the component instincts of sadism–masochism and scoptophilia–exhibitionism.

Reversal of the instinctual derivative into its opposite may explain psychotic phenomena of the following kind.

A female patient's erotomania was replaced by a persecutory delusion. She claimed that the man she believed loved her, now hated her because she had frustrated him sexually and rejected him. Despite this she insisted that his sexual desire continued unabated. This was another reason for his hating her. When she saw him she could see the lust in his eyes. She was now the object rather that the source of the sexual excitement (active to passive; love to hate).

In the following case of a character neurosis, the analytic work disclosed that a change had affected the sexual component instincts of sadism and exhibitionism in so far as they had been turned round upon the self. This necessitated the introduction of a new subject. The sexual aim (active) remained the same. It was a masturbatory phantasy that exposed the interplay between the self and objects concerned with the expression of the sadistic and exhibitionistic wish fantasies.

The patient was an unmarried woman aged 25 years. She entered analysis because of a profound sense of inferiority, shyness, and "social anxiety". She was greatly disturbed by a compulsive urge, in the presence of a man, to look at his genital region. After a long period of analysis she said that she often masturbated with the phantasy of watching a man with a very large penis penetrating a woman who was bound and tied. In adolescence she inserted her finger into her anus while masturbating. Later she substituted an object for her finger and the vagina for the anus. Masturbation was accompanied by a pleasurable sensation in the urethra. In childhood she would retain urine in order to evoke clitoral sensations. Sometimes this delaying to urinate led to incontinence and criticism from her mother. The clitoral sensations disappeared in late childhood, but she was inclined to become incontinent of urine whenever she became excited or was playing with other children. She would be overcome with embarrassment and become reluctant to mix with others in case she had an "accident". This was an important source of her "social anxiety". As a small child she tried to urinate standing up as her two younger brothers did. The crushing failure did not extinguish her conscious wish to be a boy.

In this case sadistic (masculine) and exhibitionistic sexual aims were turned on the self. A new subject was introduced as a substitute for the self. This subject, the man with the large penis, became the vehicle for these active sexual aims. She played the parts of the sadistic man and the masochistic woman. Like the sadism, the sexual aim of being looked at by an object had fallen under a taboo. As a result the wish to be looked at (exhibitionism) had been replaced by the wish to look. Looking was a feature of the masturbatory phantasy, but here too a new subject (the man with the large penis) had to be introduced so that the exhibitionism could find expression. In adult life she was unable to take pleasure in being admired by men. Instead, she was burdened by the intolerable compulsion to look at the genital region.

IV

Severe depressive states provided Freud (1917e) with phenomena that were to play a major role in his new schema of the mental apparatus. First were the changes in the ego (self) of individuals who became seriously depressed following the loss of a love object. Close scrutiny of the patients' thinking and behaviour shows that they had assimilated mental and physical characteristics of the lost object. As Freud (1917e) came to appreciate, the self-reproaches of these patients were in fact reproaches against the love object for abandoning him/her or criticisms that the patient had once directed against the love object. Identification with the lost object brought about the change from reproaches of the object to reproaching the self.

This discovery provided an understanding of specific details of the symptomatology.

A patient, a woman of 40 years, presented symptoms of depression of mood, self-blame, and signs of psychomotor retardation. Her father had died three years previously. Shortly afterwards she had a miscarriage. At the time she had thought, "You will pay for this someday." She was convinced she had induced the miscarriage by overexertion. Following her father's death, her relationship with her father-in-law, a widower, deteriorated badly. She found him unbearable, and she was instrumental in having him admitted to an old people's home.

Soon after this she developed chest pain and breathlessness. There was no organic cause for this. These were the symptoms her father had complained of in his terminal illness. Since his death she had only good memories of him and wished that he were alive. She also complained of uncomfortable abdominal sensations, which she likened to the movements of a foetus in the womb. She had identified with her father and internalized him along with the foetus—both were identified with one another. Now she unconsciously feared they would destroy her, as she had psychically destroyed them. This fear was displaced on to her husband and sons in the form of a dread that her state of mind would destroy them. Her rejection of her father-in-law had reawakened the hatred that had been caused by her father's abandonment of her through death. At the same time her wish that her father were alive and that she were pregnant was fulfilled.

Depressive states occur outwith the experience of real object loss. They too are characterized by self-criticism. This provided Freud with further evidence that a "critical agency" exists within the self and is to be distinguished as such—"What we are here becoming acquainted with is the agency commonly called conscience; we shall count it, along with the censorship of consciousness and reality testing, among the major institutions of the ego" (Freud, 1917e).

In the case of patients whose depression does not follow object loss, the content of the self-criticisms consists of plaints of having failed to meet the responsibilities of family and work, of having failed to achieve ambitions and maintain ethical standards. The inappropriate nature of the self-criticism is obvious to the on-looker, but not to the patient. While these criticisms are criticisms against others turned against the self, they are related to the patients' ideals. The self-criticisms have obtained a (psychical) reality because the critical agency has deprived the self of the satisfactions previously gained from the attainment of these ideals. Depressive states exhibit in an exaggerated manner the interaction that normally exists between the ideals and the critical agency within the self. A function of the critical agency is to ensure that the standard of the ego ideals is maintained. As long as this is so, (narcissistic) satisfaction accrues to the self and self-regard does not suffer.

Mental pathology makes it clear that the critical agency has resulted from a process of differentiation within the ego (self). It is not an innate characteristic of the ego and is therefore vulnerable to the danger of dissolution. This occurs in patients who initially fall ill with a severe depression. As time goes by the self-reproaches and the sense of guilt disappear, to be replaced by ideas of reference with a critical content. At this stage of the illness the guilt that was primarily present and expressed in self-criticism is absent. The critical agency within the ego has disappeared and been replaced by criticism from outside the self. The patient feels himself to be unjustly accused.

A man aged 46 years, married with two children, became severely depressed. He was forever criticizing himself for a variety of shortcomings. He was suicidal. He gradually improved with the aid of medications. A few months later there was a relapse with similar symptoms. Slowly the depressive mood lifted and the self-criticism abated. Instead he became suspicious. He believed he was under surveillance by unknown individuals. He believed he was being followed and all his actions observed. He then reported that he heard a voice calling him a cheat and a liar. He had come to the conclusion that his persecutors were intent on demonstrating and proving that he had committed a crime.

There was, in this case, sufficient data to suggest that the crime he had psychically committed was killing his mother, who died three months before the first attack. Unconscious death wishes had acted as the immediate instigator of the attack.

Cases of this type led Freud (1921c) to state that the differentiation of a mental function from the basic psychical matrix creates the potential for pathological developments—"Each of the mental differentiations . . . represents a fresh aggravation of the difficulties of mental functioning, increases its instability, and may become a starting point for its breakdown, that is, for the onset of a disease" (Freud, 1921c).

V

In *Group Psychology and the Analysis of the Ego*, Freud (1921c) hypothesizes that the physical act of oral incorporation is the prototype for the psychical internalization (introjection) that leads to identification. This hypothesis was to have powerful repercussions not only with regard to Freud's theory of the structure of the ego (1923b) but for later psychoanalytic theorizing. The ambivalence that is inherent in the wish to be the same as another was instrumental in leading Freud to follow Abraham (1924) and discern a destructive element in oral incorporation. Thus Freud (1921c) writes—"Identification is ambivalent from the very first; it can turn into an expression of tenderness as easily as in fact, into a wish for someone's removal. It behaves like a derivative of the first, oral phase of the organization of the libido, in which the object that we long for and prize is assimilated by eating and is in that way annihilated as such."

In addition to the different psychical conditions that lead to identification—wish-fulfilment and regression from object choice—Freud (1921c) added a third. Identification occurs when there is a common quality shared with another person. Identification also serves the purpose of defence. By replacing object choice, the dangers that may come to be associated with the choice are removed. Freud (1923b) came to regard this process as of the greatest importance in creating the constitution of the structural ego. In some dreams, identification with a parental figure brings about the "repression" of memories of violent and sexual acts between the parents. Identification with the perpetrator of the violence ensures the absence of anxiety and protects sleep. This is comparable to the play of children who, through identification with parents, "remember" incidents of a similar kind. An understanding of specific contents of persecutory delusions is possible when there is an awareness of the extent to which perception of the self is altered by identification acting as a defence. In cases of paranoid schizophrenia and paranoid psychosis, the patient believes that he/she is being slandered by a known person of the same sex—that he/she is promiscuous, etc. In the case of a male patient, the persecutor is believed to be virile and sought out by women. In the case of a female patient, the persecutor is believed to be the object of male admiration with many conquests to her credit. In the pre-illness (pre-psychotic) period both male and female patients are envious of the persecutors-to-be. In becoming the envied man/woman (wish fulfilled), the unconscious homosexuality is disposed of and heterosexuality confirmed. However, the envy and hatred remain, but projected. The patient is now slandered in his new "persona", as he once wished to slander the envied object.

Identification is not the only process that leads to changes in the way the self is perceived. In *Group Psychology and the Analysis of the Ego*, Freud (1921c) designates the critical agency within the ego that underwrites moral conscience, the censorship of dreams, self-observation and repression, as the ego-ideal. Observations of the mentally healthy as well as in the mentally ill show that the ego-ideal can alter either in the direction of overactivity or lose its power altogether. In the state of being in love there is an overvaluation of the beloved. This is comparable to the overvaluation of the persecutor in persecutory types of psychosis. In both, the self is depleted and powerless. When in love, the individual ego has given over its self-love to the beloved. The dissolution of the critical agency (the ego-ideal) that occurs in this state leads to an uncritical acceptance of the wishes of the beloved. "The object has been put in the place of the ego-ideal" (Freud, 1921c). The way in which the self is perceived and acts thus depends on the state of the ego-ideal.

VI

The changes that affect the self (ego) and object in their interrelationships can be classified according to whether the self has become a substitute for the object or the object has become a substitute for the self—either in whole or in part. The former (self for object) includes the transitivism, where the self assumes features of mental and physical aspects of the object; the depreciated self substituting for the object in cases of depression that follow object loss; in scoptophilia, where the looking substitutes for being looked at (exhibitionism); and in homosexuality, where the self becomes the mother of childhood. The latter includes erotomania, transitivism (where the object in endowed with aspects of the self), delusional jealousy (a type of homosexuality in which the object is the wished-for self), and the state of being in love.

When these substitutions of self for object and object for self are examined as to cause, it becomes apparent that wish-fulfilment and the psychical reactions that this engenders play the major roles. These reactions frequently obscure the underlying wish-fulfilment, as in the case of the transformation of exhibitionism into scoptophilia; the guilt caused by death-wishes, which leads to the self-reproaches in depressive states; and the anxiety that occurs in the transitivism where admired and wished-for characteristics of the object are assimilated into the self. Against this is the straightforward wish-fulfilment that occurs in the transitivism where the object is altered in accordance with features of the self, as in maniacal states and acute schizophrenic attacks.

The new schema of the mental apparatus

I

In the new schema of the mental apparatus as described in *The Ego and the Id*, the systems of that apparatus (primary and secondary processes) are overshadowed by Freud's (1923b) concentration on the functions of ego, superego, and id and how they are influenced by "The Two Classes of Instincts". The ego is now regarded as part of the self and not identical with it—"We have formed the idea that in each individual there is a coherent organization of mental processes; and we call this his ego" (Freud, 1923b). Consciousness, logical verbal thinking, control of motility, reflective awareness, perception, memory, and reality testing are functions of this ego. So is repression. The ego concept thus embraces all the functions previously attributed to the secondary process—the secondary system (Freud, 1900a). The phenomena of unconscious resistance that reflect the action of repression require that the ego must also have an unconscious element no less (dynamically) unconscious than the repressed.

The nucleus of the ego, Freud (1923b) proposed, was the (topographical) system (*Pcpt–Cs*), which is in receipt of external stimuli and stimuli that arise from within the interior of the mental apparatus. External stimuli are registered but may not be perceived consciously. This is demonstrated through dream analysis, tachistoscopic experiments, and by the disruption of purposive thought by percepts in psychotic patients (Freeman, 1965). How internal stimuli reach consciousness can only be hypothesized about. According to the theory of the pleasure principle, internal stimuli become conscious if they do not evoke unpleasure. As these internal stimuli "represent displacements of mental energy" (Freud, 1923b), they must make connections with the memory traces of words if they are to obtain the potential for consciousness. As word presentations, derived from auditory perceptions, are located in the system *Pcs* along with memory (verbal) schemata, that system (*Pcs*) is part of the (structural) ego.

Freud (1923b) followed Groddeck in naming the system unconscious the id. Like that system the id is the source of the life and death instincts. In the first theory (Freud, 1900a), the system unconscious included the repressed, the unconscious elements of the self and its critical faculty. The id, speaking topographically, is now the site of these mental processes. Like the system unconscious the id is more than the repressed. The antithesis conscious—unconscious was now replaced by the antithesis of the ego and the repressed.

That the replacement of object choice (object cathexes) by identification is an ubiquitous psychical event is shown by the clinical phenomena that have been referred to here (see p. 58), as forerunners of the theory of psychical structures (ego and superego). Identification now achieved prominence as the means whereby the ego was constituted. The psychical internalization (introjection) of an object was now regarded as oral in nature. With identification sexual aims directed to the object are abandoned. With this abandonment, object libido is assimilated into the ego and transformed into narcissistic libido. Identification thus results in desexualization—a kind of sublimation (Freud, 1923b). Freud does not explicitly address the question of the source of the energy that the ego uses to carry out its different functions. There is the implication that the cathexes drawn into the ego from objects, in the course of identification, must contribute to this.

The critical agency within the self becomes the superego (Freud, 1923b). An important question had to be answered—what is the source of the power that enables the superego to dominate the ego? Here the theory of life (libido) and death instincts is crucial. Freud (1923b) begins his explanation, first, with patients who react to analysis with a negative therapeutic reaction, and second, with those who suffer from obsessional neuroses and depressive states. Patients who exhibit a negative therapeutic reaction are free of conscious guilt. Those with obsessional neuroses and depressive states are plagued by guilt. This follows from the oppression of the ego by the superego. Freud (1923b) theorized as follows—the death instinct had possessed the superego resulting in the free expression of sadism (a sadistic superego). How is the death instinct set free? Ordinarily the "dangerous death instinct" (Freud, 1923b) is fused with the libido. A defusion has occurred in obsessional neuroses and depressive states concomitant with instinctual regression.

Freud (1923b) theorizes that ordinarily the superego obtains its power to criticize the ego from the death instinct, which is no longer fused with libido. It is the identifications that form the core of the superego that are responsible for this defusion. Identification leads to desexualization (see above), thus leaving the libido insufficient energy to maintain its fusion with the death instinct. On the basis of this theorizing, Freud (1923b) concluded that the purpose of the desexualization that occurs *pari passu* with the establishment of the (oedipal) identifications (superego) is to enable the ego to assist the death instinct in its task of controlling the erotic (life) instincts. However, in carrying out this function, the ego is faced with the danger of becoming the object of the death instinct. This comes to pass in the obsessional neuroses and depressive states. To offset this danger the ego is in constant need of libidinal reinforcement. As Freud (1923b) states—". . . it thus itself (the ego) becomes the representative of Eros and henceforth desires to live and be loved".

II

As Freud's later writings make explicit (Freud, 1933a, 1940a), the introduction of the concepts of ego, id, and superego did not alter his basic theory of the mental apparatus (Freud, 1900a). The energy available to the ego to carry out its functions (the economic aspect) comprised those cathexes that had been bound and altered in their quality by the secondary process. The functions of the ego were those previously attributed to the secondary system (*Pcs*), especially the automatic restriction on the build-up of unpleasure (repression, the dynamic aspect). Although the ego is differentiated from the id and operates according to the secondary process, mobile id cathexes can be released, when appropriate, from inhibitory restraint, finding representation in thoughts and actions that have wish-fulfilment as their aim. Thus the ego remains under the influence of the pleasure principle in either its positive (discharge) or negative (inhibitory) aspects.

To repeat, Freud's (1923b) theory of the superego in its genetic, dynamic, economic, and topographic dimensions leans heavily on the "dual theory of the instincts". He had doubts about the theory, as the following quotation illustrates—"There is, it is true, no doubt about the pleasure principle and the differentiation within the ego has good clinical justification, but the distinction between the two classes of instinct does not seem sufficiently assured and it is possible that the facts of clinical analysis may be found which will do away with its pretension" (Freud, 1923b). Despite this, he reached for clinical phenomena that promised support for the theory. He singled out the fact that love can turn into hate and hate into love. Earlier, Freud (1915c) had rejected the idea that this was the result of a transformation of affect. He had identified unpleasure, caused by external and internal stimuli, as the fore-runner of hate being a reaction of the self-preservative instinct. The introduction of the theory of the two classes of instinct precluded the possibility of a transformation of affect because Eros and the death instinct were qualitatively different from one another. To get around this, Freud (1923b) turned to those cases of persecutory paranoia where the persecutor was a formerly loved and admired person. The apparent transformation of affect, he theorized, was brought about by cathexes being withdrawn from the libidinal (life) instincts and displaced on to the death instincts. This concept of a displaceable energy, "neutral in itself" (Freud, 1923b), could explain how hatred may replace love—the death instinct height-ened at the expense of the life instinct.

If a reason is to be found to account for Freud's introduction of the theory of the two classes of instinct and the structural concepts, it must surely have been his need to find an explanation for the fact that severe cases of obsessional neuroses, depressive states, and disorders of personality so often proved refractory to the psycho-analytic treatment method. The theory of an unconscious superego suffused with the death instinct offered an explanation for the negative therapeutic reaction. In turning to theorizing in this way, Freud set a fashion in psychoanalysis. The history of psychoanaly-sis shows (see Chapters 6, 7, 8, and 9) that the failure to achieve therapeutic success has led many analysts to reinterpret clinical phenomena in terms of newly devised theoretical concepts and subsequently change their therapeutic technique.

CHAPTER FIVE

A short detour
around Freud's theories of anxiety

I

In "Inhibitions, Symptoms and Anxiety" Freud (1926d) reformulated his first theory of anxiety in accord with the revised concept of the mental apparatus. In the new theory, a disturbance of libido economics is no longer regarded as the principal source of anxiety. Instead the ego organization (Freud, 1923b) is the regulator of anxiety. Anxiety is not created automatically each time libidinal cathexes are unable to find an outlet in reality. In the new theory, the energy necessary to produce the unpleasure of anxiety is disconnected from the cathexis of a repressed (libidinal) impulse. Rather, anxiety is a reproduced affective state—"It (anxiety) is reproduced as an affective state in accordance with an already existing mnemic image" (Freud, 1926d). Anxiety, like other affective states, Freud (1926d) speculates, ". . . has become incorporated in the mind as precipitates of primeval traumatic experiences".

According to the new theory, anxiety is evoked by a situation identified as dangerous by the ego (Freud, 1926d). The response to an internal danger created by unacceptable wishes or the superego

71

is modelled on that which occurs in situations of external danger—repression in the former, flight in the latter. Anxiety is the stimulus for repression. In contrast to the first theory, repression does not lead to anxiety through the transformation of the cathexis of an instinctual derivative. With anxiety separated from the libido, Freud (1926d) described a number of internal danger situations that may lead to the expression of that affect. Anxiety may be a response to fear of the superego, of the id (destructive as well as libidinal instincts), to separation, and to real external danger.

In turning to the question of "What anxiety really is", Freud (1926d) puts aside the new psychological considerations (ego as the seat of anxiety, etc.) and reverts to the economic concepts that are basic to his theory of mind (1900a, 1915c, 1915e). His attention is turned to the connections which may exist between anxiety and somatic processes. By way of illustration he cites the instance of the hungry infant. In this state he envisages (Freud, 1926d) a build-up of excitations within the mental apparatus which can neither be dealt with psychically nor discharged in an act of satisfaction. An analogous situation is the acute stage of a traumatic neurosis (see Chapter 3). In the case of the infant, only the mother can satisfy the infant's hunger, so reducing the level of excitation and restoring psychical equilibrium. The mother's absence at the time of need creates a danger—the threat of an economic catastrophe. When the infant comes to connect the mother's presence and the relief of hunger, the danger is transferred from the economic condition (build-up of excitation within the mental apparatus) to the circumstance that provoked this condition—namely, the absence of the mother. Object loss or the threat of object loss (separation) now constitutes the danger situation. This must be avoided to prevent a revival of the potential economic catastrophe.

As development proceeds the infant gradually extricates himself from the automatic (economic) reaction to object loss. Anxiety now comes under the control of the emerging ego and acts as a signal to anticipate the danger of a traumatic situation occurring. This formulation allowed Freud (1926d) to reconcile the economic hypothesis with the new (psychological) theory of anxiety. Here the first, involuntary response to object loss is replaced by an adaptive, self-preservative reaction. Complete helplessness is replaced by increasing mastery over the threat of an impending danger. Signal anxiety is contrasted with traumatic anxiety—"Anxiety is the original reaction to helplessness in a trauma and is reproduced later on in the danger situation as a signal for help" (Freud, 1926d). The reaction to object loss is the prototype for all later danger situations—castration fear and fear of the superego and of the id.

II

The clinical phenomena that led Freud (1895b, 1917d) to construct his first theory of anxiety present themselves in clinical work. One form of this is illustrated in the following example.

A man of 32 years, previously healthy and potent, complained of tachycardia and breathlessness. The symptoms had been present for several months. He feared he had heart disease but was not helped by the fact that there was no defect in his cardiovascular system. He was married with two children, the younger being one year old. In the course of psychotherapy he revealed that following the birth of his second child he had begun to practise coitus interruptus because neither he nor his wife wanted another child. He did not discuss the matter of contraception with his wife because he thought that she would be embarrassed. The limited satisfaction he obtained from coitus interruptus gradually disappeared, leaving him without sexual desire. The anxiety symptoms followed. When he was able to acknowledge that it was he who had difficulty in talking about sexual matters, he and his wife were able to follow a contraceptive regime that led to the return of his sexual desire and potency. The symptoms disappeared. At follow-up some two years later he remained well. His choice of symptom could be traced to his mother, who had suffered from rheumatic disease of the heart and had died from heart failure.

This case falls into Freud's (1895b) category of an actual or contemporary neurosis. Such cases, although not so common nowadays, are particularly impressive because of the temporal association between the loss of sexual potency and anxiety symptoms.

The same temporal association is regularly encountered in cases of anxiety hysteria. For example:

A married man fell ill with an acute anxiety that manifested itself in chest pain and tremulousness. There was no sign of heart disease. He became so afraid of experiencing the symptoms that he was afraid to leave the house. He had been an energetic, ambitious man who had succeeded in his business life. Although fond of his wife, he had come to find her unexciting and unsatisfying. He began a relationship with another woman, which afforded him intense pleasure. His first attack occurred when he was with his woman friend. He feared he was about to die. From that time on his sexual desire was extinguished. He became dependent on his wife and gave up the relationship with the woman.

Here the choice of symptom was based on the fact that his older brother had died of a heart attack about a year previously.

A transient but sometimes permanent loss of sexual desire and potency associated with anxiety symptoms is found in men whose wives are pregnant (Freeman, 1951). When these men present themselves at a psychiatric clinic there is an opportunity to detect this connection and examine it. More often than not the patient's history shows that the mother or some close female relative either died or was taken seriously ill during pregnancy or labour. Ambivalence resulting from envy and jealousy of the unborn child (Reik, 1936) and the fact of sexual frustration also contribute to this. In some cases the patient may admit to the phantasy that coitus will kill the foetus. A combination of libidinal frustration and unconscious death wishes may be proposed as the instigators of the patient's symptoms. In these cases the loss of sexual desire is matched by the appearance of symptoms of anxiety.

A further instance of the association between loss of sexual desire and anxiety is provided by anxiety dreams that follow coitus. These dreams are regularly encountered during the analytic treatment of character neuroses as well as of symptom neuroses. The initial content of these typical dreams is of an exciting and pleasurable nature—driving a car at high speed, riding a bicycle down a hill, flying, engaging in some dangerous exploit (espionage etc.). At a certain point the excitement changes into anxiety, and the patient fears for his life. The car is about to crash, or those on whom he has been spying are about to attack him. The important fact about these dreams is that they occur after an unsatisfying coitus for which there are various external reasons—one of the partners suddenly experiences pain leading him or her to break off the coitus, premature emission on the part of the man, etc. What is striking is that the content of the dream parallels the coital experiences so closely—excitement followed by the unpleasure of frustration. The dream is a memory of the unsatisfying coitus.

In the case of these post-coital dreams and in the other instances described, it is possible to explain the anxiety on purely psychological grounds in accordance with Freud's (1926d) second theory of anxiety. The frustration leads to unconscious death wishes against the frustrating partner. A danger situation is created and anxiety follows. This explanation does not take account of what happens to the sexual excitement—the quota of affect— which disappears from consciousness. Repression has not succeeded in its primary function—that is, the removal of unpleasure, now in the form of anxiety. As described above, Freud's (1895b) first theory was that the libidinal cathexis, repeatedly denied an outlet in real satisfaction, was directly transformed into anxiety. An unknown pathophysiological process was invoked as the cause. All that remained in consciousness of the sexual affect consisted of an exaggerated physiological accompaniment (anxiety equivalents). The sexual affect had been repressed. It followed that repression led to anxiety. However for repression to occur, a sufficient "energy" was required to keep the sexual affect from consciousness. This energy, Freud (1915d) proposed, was borrowed from the libidinal cathexes (the sexual affect). But how does this take place? The second theory of anxiety (Freud, 1926d) resolves this difficult question by dispensing with the economic explanation and instead accords the ego the function of signalling anxiety in the face of a danger situation.

It follows from the second theory of anxiety that in abnormal mental states, where there are intense anxiety affects, the ego has lost its signal function. The sense of helplessness that the patient experiences shows that the anxiety has a traumatic quality akin to that hypothesized for the infant (Freud, 1926d). This sense of helplessness is present in schizophrenic psychoses at acute onset and during acute attacks in chronicity. The connection between sexual excitement, expressed directly or in sadistic terms, is clear to see when exciting phantasies (delusions) are replaced by anxiety (e.g. when erotomania is replaced by persecutory delusions). The conscious reactions of these patients stand in complete contrast to those patients whose anxiety symptoms have no obvious connection with conscious sexual conflict, as for example in those women who are vaginally anaesthetic or men who are impotent.

III

In presenting his second theory of anxiety, Freud (1926d) states it is not "... so much a matter of taking back earlier findings as bringing them into line with more recent discoveries". Although he does not specify what these recent discoveries are, they cannot be unconnected with the theory of the life and death instincts (Freud, 1920g) and the structural formulations (Freud, 1923b). The theory of the life and death instincts required more that a revision of the first theory of anxiety. It had to be replaced entirely. Unsatisfied libido could no longer be regarded as the principal cause of morbid anxiety. Previously aggression, as expressed in death wishes (Freud, 1900a), had been attributed to the ego instincts. With sadism and aggression now expressions of the death instinct, they must constitute a primary cause of danger and thus of anxiety. Equally the ego had to have a role in the creation of anxiety. Klein (1932) followed Freud here in her theory that the first and only source of anxiety is the derivatives of the death instinct.

Fundamental for the second theory is the assumption that the reaction to an internal (psychical) danger is modelled on the reaction to an external danger. Is this equivalence justified by the observable data? Is there only a quantitative difference between realistic and morbid anxiety? The significant difference that exists between the anxiety that the mentally healthy experience in the face of an external danger and the anxiety experienced by those suffering from neuroses and psychoses was ignored by Freud (1926d), in contrast to the emphasis placed on them in his earlier work (Freud, 1895b, 1916–17). The reaction to an external danger consists of a conscious feeling of fear and somatic accompaniments of varying degrees of severity. Purposive acts may be initiated to counter this danger.

In the case of those who suffer from anxiety hysteria, the anxiety is expressed predominantly through the body. These patients fear re-experiencing the physical symptoms that attended the acute onset of the illness (i.e. the first anxiety attack). They fear the recurrence of faintness, tachycardia, palpitations, breathlessness, the precipitate need to micturate or defaecate. They take every precaution (phobia formation) to avoid this, particularly those situations where the first attack occurred (see Mr A, Chapter 2—a typical case of anxiety hysteria). The nature of the anxiety is different from that experienced by a healthy person when faced with a real danger, in so far as the patient does not primarily experience conscious fear. The fear follows the expectation and experience of the physical expressions of the anxiety.

Anxiety dreams and the anxiety that is part of persecutory delusions have much more in common with the reaction to a real external danger. The schizophrenic or paranoid patient fears an attack on his mind or body, and this leads to a sense of helplessness that is akin to that experienced by an individual who is traumatized by real danger. The pathological phenomena suggest that if the reaction to an external danger is to be taken as the model for the reaction to an internal danger, then it has validity only when the reaction is one of helplessness (i.e. is traumatic).

The fact that different forms of anxiety exist must have played a part in causing Freud (1926d) to hesitate before abandoning the economic hypothesis with its basis in somatic processes. Is the anxiety caused by a real danger, even when it leads to a sense of helplessness, identical in nature to the anxiety experienced in neurotic and psychotic states? At one point Freud (1926d) is quite definite in his rejection of the economic hypothesis, for he writes— "I formerly believed that anxiety invariably arose automatically by an economic process, my present conception of anxiety as a signal given by the ego in order to affect the pleasure–unpleasure agency does away with the necessity of considering the economic factor." Yet later in the same work reservations appear. These suggest that he had difficulty in renouncing the theory that morbid anxiety is the response of instinctual cathexes that have been subject to repression. He writes (Freud, 1926d)—"It cannot be denied that the libido belonging to the id processes is subject to disturbances at the instigation of repression. It might still be true therefore, that in repression anxiety is produced from the libidinal cathexis of the instinctual impulse." Is it the ego alone from which anxiety arises in abnormal mental states? This seems unlikely when the ego is weakened or disorganized, as it is in these conditions.

In perceiving a similarity between the morbid anxiety that occurs in abnormal mental states and the anxiety experienced by healthy individuals when confronted by a real danger, Freud (1926d) appears to suggest that these affective responses belong in a continuum. One is just an exaggerated (pathological) form of the other. This view is reminiscent of the theory (Freud, 1917e) that severe depressive states (melancholia) that follow object loss are a pathological variant of the state of mourning. The symptomatology and course of illness of severe depressions point to a qualitative difference between these conditions and the state of mourning. Morbid anxiety of mental disorders may be quite different in nature when compared to the reactions to real danger even when the reaction is inexpedient.

A theory of anxiety that disconnects itself from somatic processes necessitates the exclusion of the economic dimension. This ignores the likelihood that a qualitative difference exists between the anxiety displayed in the course of mental illness (neuroses and psychoses) and the anxiety that arises in the mentally healthy when they are faced with real danger.

CHAPTER SIX

The reinterpretation
of clinical facts (descriptive data)

I

Those who have introduced different concepts and theories into psychoanalysis (Bion, 1959, 1962; Fairbairn, 1944; Klein, 1932, 1935, 1946; Kohut, 1971, 1977) may rightly claim that the sources are to be found in Freud's later (1919–1923) writings. The content of Chapters 3, 4, and 5 illustrates this. The fundamental role of destructiveness in psychical life postulated by Klein is based on Freud's theory of the death instinct. The theory of hallucinatory gratification (see Chapter 1) has been used to support the concept of unconscious phantasy (Klein, 1935, 1940), though it belongs to a different theoretical discourse. The central position of ego–object interactions (object relations) in the theories of Klein and Fairbairn is a logical extension and development of the explanatory concepts described by Freud in "Mourning and Melancholia" (1917e), *Group Psychology and the Analysis of the Ego* (1921c), and *The Ego and the Id* (1923b) (see Chapter 4).

It is impossible to detect antecedents for these alternative theories in Freud's theory of normal and pathological mental life as outlined in the seventh chapter of *The Interpretation of Dreams*

(1900a) and in the metapsychological papers (1916–17). The exception here is the theory of hallucinatory gratification as mentioned above. The core of Freud's theory (see Chapter 1) consists of a formulation that explains the prevalence of wishing, of substitute formations as occur in dreams, in parapraxes, and in the content of neurotic and psychotic symptoms, as explained in terms of the concept of the primary process (see Chapter 1). Mobile cathexes are displaced from the mental representations of the self, objects, memories, words, etc., to other representations in the search for wish-fulfilment. For example, a woman's repressed wish to enjoy the pleasures of eating finds a substitute in the pleasure gained from encouraging her child to eat. A wish is fulfilled through displacement of cathexis from self to child.

This dynamic–economic theory (see Chapter 1) has been replaced by a structural model of mind that has at its hub the interactions of the ego and its objects (psychical structures). This theory advanced originally by Klein and Fairbairn provides an alternative interpretation of the phenomena of psychical wish-fulfilment, wishing, and substitute formations. Psychical wish-fulfilment is subsumed under the concept of omnipotence. Wish-fulfilment follows omnipotence as it affects the ego, part and whole objects (see Chapters 7 and 10). Omnipotence may be destructive or reparative (Klein, 1932). Reparative omnipotence reduces anxiety and guilt caused by destructive attacks on the object. In replacing wish-fulfilment by omnipotence, Freud's (1900a) theory of the wish as an irreducible element of mental life and as an expression of the pleasure principle is dispensed with. A consequence of this is that the concept of psychical wish-fulfilment has virtually disappeared from the vocabulary of Kleinian terms.

Substitute formations are also explained in a different way. They are interpreted as the result of an active process of psychical splitting (a schizoid process) that affects the ego and it objects. For example, a figure in a dream is shown by analysis to represent an unacceptable aspect of the self. This, according to the "schizoid" theory, follows from the splitting of the dreamer's ego into two parts—one conscious and acceptable, the other unacceptable. Object representations may also be split, as in a dream where one object represents an admired or loved individual and the other one who is feared and hated. In this way (i.e. through splitting) hatred of the admired figure is denied access to the dream consciousness (a defence).

For Klein (1946) and Fairbairn (1944), psychical splitting is a fundamental characteristic of mind. Splitting, it is claimed, is present from the earliest period of mental development. The primitive ego lacks integration and thus is liable to fragmentation. As development proceeds, there is a progressive integration of the self and its contents. However the tendency to fragment (split) is constantly present. In Fairbairn's theory the tendency for the rudimentary ego to split is increased when the infant suffers frustration and disappointment at the hands of the mother. The representation of an unempathic mother—the breast (a part object, see Chapter 7)—is then split into a "good", satisfying object and a "bad", frustrating object. Only the latter is internalized (introjected), so that reasonable relations are maintained with the mother in reality. Klein (1946) follows Freud's (1923b) theory that quantities of the death instinct existing within the ego must be externalized in order to preserve its integrity. Klein (1932, 1935, 1946) does not always differentiate clearly between the concept of self and the ego organization (Freud, 1923b). Ego and self seem to be used interchangeably.

According to Klein (1946), splitting of the ego is caused by the death instinct, but this very splitting permits the externalization of those elements of the ego that contain the death instinct. This takes the form of destructive attacks on the breast (part object), which is then also split. Splitting of the object allows the representation of the "good" satisfying breast to be kept apart from the unsatisfying "bad" breast. In contrast to Fairbairn's theory, both "good" and "bad" breasts are internalized. In advocating splitting and projection of "bits" of the ego (projective identification) to account for the externalization of the death instinct, Klein shows her preference for the theory of mind in which the structural dimension is preeminent. Splitting (the schizoid process) provides an explanation for the phenomena that Freud (1900a, 1915c, 1917d) attributed to the action of the primary process with its aim of wish-fulfilment.

The case of Mr A described in Chapter 2 may be taken to illustrate how the psychoanalytic clinical facts that emerged in his analysis may be interpreted according to the theory of splitting of the self and objects. In terms of the theories of Klein and Fairbairn the neurosis resulted from an unconscious conflict between the "good" and "bad" parts of the self. The libido plays a secondary role here that is principally limited to psychical acts of reparation (see above). Mr A's dependency on his wife after the onset of the neurosis, and on the author, reflected his need to have good objects that would reinforce and protect the "good" parts of the self. His fear of entrapment (the phobic anxiety) was the result of the action of the "bad" parts of the self, expressed in acquisitive sexual greed (the immediate cause of the neurosis) and in the omnipotent sadistic (fox and spider) phantasies. These were split off and projected into objects, making them "bad" and "persecutory"—hence the morbid fear of people. Envy of the woman (originally the mother) and the need to possess her "goodness" had damaged her. A psychically damaged mother was introjected, resulting in an identification with her (the symptom of shakiness). The neurosis erupted because of the inability to stave off the destructive attacks on the mother. This would have allowed omnipotent reparative tendencies (manic defence, see Chapter 7) to restore her integrity.

The concept of splitting or schizoid process (the two terms are interchangeable) offers an opportunity to illustrate the manner in which what was originally a descriptive concept comes to possess an explanatory role. As Fairbairn (1940) writes, the concept ". . . schizoid has the inestimable advantage that it is not simply descriptive, but is explanatory in a psychogenetic sense". Does the history of the concept justify and support this claim?

The history of the schizoid concept is at variance with the view that the schizoid condition implies the action of an active process of psychical splitting. The schizoid concept had its origins ". . . in connection with the expression 'schizophrenic' around 1910" (Bleuler, 1978) at Burghölzli in Zurich. Kretchmer (1918) described a type of personality that he called schizoid because of its similarity to the pre-psychotic personality of many schizophrenic patients—i.e. oversensitive, unpredictable, aloof, stubborn, and affectively labile. Fairbairn (1940) identified these traits in some of his patients and designated them as schizoid personality types (see Chapter 10). "Schizoid" seemed to Kretchmer (1918) a suitable term to describe this personality type because of the dissociations (splitting) that existed in different spheres of their mental functioning—e.g. the divorce of affect from thought, phantasying divorced from reality, etc. Splitting described facets of a particular (schizoid) type of personality.

II

The concept of psychical splitting begins with Janet (1893). He introduced it to describe the presence of clinical phenomena (twilight amnesic states, somnambulism, multiple personality, and motor and sensory symptoms) that he attributed to an altered state of consciousness. During attacks the patient was no longer himself. He was inaccessible and uninfluencible. Janet (1893) described these manifestations as mental automatisms (the involuntary expression of thoughts, intentions, affects, and motor acts). He concluded that the clinical phenomena were the result of a weakness in the patient's field of consciousness. It is important to remember here that the concept of the field of consciousness is something more than the capacity to orientate the self to time, place, and person. It, the field of consciousness, consists of voluntary thought and action, the cognitive functions that serve environmental adaptation and affect control—similar to Freud's ego organization.

The lowering of the level of the field of consciousness [abaissement du niveau mental] leads to ideation, affect, and actions leaving the main stream of consciousness. During an hysterical attack the patient has lost the capacity to integrate and unify cognition, affect, and conation. The function of psychical synthesis is no longer operative. It was this lack that permitted the dissociation (the splitting off) of specific ideational and affective complexes. Achieving an autonomy, they come to dominate mental life. Dissociation or splitting of mental life is thus secondary to the lowering of the level of the field of consciousness.

Freud (1894a) followed Janet in acknowledging that an altered state of consciousness existed in cases of hysteria distinct from that of the mentally healthy. His own observations led him to reject the theory of the "abaissement du niveau mental". Splitting or dissociation existed, but Freud initially (1894a) proposed that this was the result of an act of will on the patient's part. Behavioural manifestations and physical symptoms, he concluded, arose when a wish or memory led to a conflict with the remainder of the personality.

These wishes or traumatic memories were no longer in the patient's awareness, not because they had lost their attachment to the field of consciousness (lack of psychical synthesis), but because they had eventually succumbed to an automatic process that Freud (1894a) described as repression. Freud (1894a) stated that "the characteristic factor in hysteria is not the splitting of consciousness but the capacity for conversion". The altered states of consciousness and physical symptoms characteristic of hysteria represented the conversion of complexes of ideas and affects incompatible with the patient's moral and ethical standards.

The concept of splitting was further developed within the context of Bleuler's (1911) theory of the schizophrenias. He introduced the concept of "systematic splitting" to describe such phenomena as "double book-keeping", the positive and negative aspects of autism, transitivism, and parathymia. "Systematic splitting" is a descriptive concept and provides the clinical basis for the concept of schizophrenia. In keeping with Janet's (1893) theory, "systematic splitting" is the result of a fundamental psychical disturbance which Bleuler (1911) described as a weakness of the processes of thought association. In Bleuler's (1911) words "Behind the systematic splitting into definite idea complexes, we have found a primary loosening of the association structure". This was caused by an unknown physical process. According to both Janet and Bleuler, the symptoms of the hysterias and the schizophrenias were the outcome of the dissolution of the highest hierarchical level of mental life. Splitting and fragmentation of mental life followed.

As far as the schizophrenias are concerned, the usage of the concept of splitting as explanatory has led to a reinterpretation of the disorder in the form of thinking that occurs in these conditions. The theory that they are in part an expression of a movement towards recovery (phase of restitution, Freud, 1911c, 1915e) is replaced. Instead, Bion (1959) proposed that the "loosening of the association structure" is caused by destructive attacks on the links between the forerunners of verbal thought, which Bion (1959) likens to ideographs (graphic signs). The result of these attacks is to destroy the links between ideographs, with adverse consequence for verbal thought. The link between the sign (verbal symbol) and the signified (object) is damaged. Through this splitting the patient protects himself from awareness of the hated and feared objects in external and internal reality (see Chapter 9).

Freud's later reference to what he called "a split in the ego" (1940e) does not contradict his original view (1894a) that splitting is a descriptive concept. Its use draws attention to the contradictory mental events that are to be observed in cases of psychosis, in hysterical and schizoid personality types, and in fetishism. Splitting (Freud, 1940e) is contingent on the rejection of specific experiences (denial) in the case of fetishism. This denial however does not interfere with the actual registration in the mind of what had been perceived (see Chapter 2). In the case of the formation of a fetish, it is not a matter of the splitting of the ego but of a rejection by the man of the woman's lack of a penis. A substitute is formed by displacement (the fetish), while the reality of her "castrated" state is consciously acknowledged.

According to Janet, Freud, and Bleuler, splitting describes clinical phenomena which show that mental and physical aspects of the self have been fragmented and thus "split off". In the theories of Klein and Fairbairn, the concept of splitting has been given an explanatory role. It is offered as an explanation for clinical phenomena. How does the splitting or fragmentation occur? What is its cause?—"What splits in splitting?" (Pruyser, 1975). The change of status from description to explanation is based on theoretical assumptions that as later chapters will show, depend on a specific type of interpretation of clinical phenomena. The theoretical assumptions are, first, that psychical splitting occurs because it is an inherent property of mental life from infancy onwards (Fairbairn) and, second, that it is caused by derivatives of the death instinct (unconscious oral–sadistic phantasies—Klein). Despite their differences with respect to the usage of splitting, Klein, Fairbairn, and Kohut, like Janet, envisage the self (ego) as a psychical structure whose essential vulnerability lies in the tendency to fragment.

The introduction of the concept of an active psychical splitting has led to an alternative explanation of phenomena that Freud (1900a) attributed to repression. Memories, wishes, and affects which, until their recovery during analytical treatment, have been unconscious are interpreted as having been split off from consciousness rather that being repressed. Splitting renders not only the concept of repression (after expulsion) superfluous, but the concept of primary repression also. Splitting accounts for the absence from consciousness of wishes, actions, and memories that were once conscious but also for those psychical events that never reach consciousness (see Chapter 2).

Sandler (1997) has subjected the concept of repression to a radical revision within the context of his theory of the past and present unconscious. Clinical experience led him to conclude that the wishes, thoughts, and phantasies that appear in analysis are not derivatives of unconscious mental events of early childhood. They arise in the analysand's current mental life as if he/she were a child with his/her particular developmental history. If the emerging mental content provokes conflict it is then subject to repression and other defences. Repression thus acts within the province of a present unconscious. It has to be applied when an internal danger arises. The past unconscious consists of what Sandler (1997) describes as "dynamic templates and rules of functioning", which create the form of the phantasies arising in the present unconscious. Repression plays no part in the past unconscious. In terms of Sandler's theory, the content of masturbatory phantasies, for example, owes nothing to primal repression of early childhood phantasies and memories of real experiences. The role of primary repression was illustrated in the case of Mr B in Chapter 2. According to Sandler (1997), the amnesia of early childhood is not caused by primal repression but by the child's limited cognitive functioning.

In confining the concept of repression to the present unconscious—that is, to the "forgetting" of events and phantasies that were once conscious—Sandler (1997) circumvents the controversy about early childhood experiences that can never be recalled ("infantile amnesia"). Sandler's theory (1997) is based on his clinical work and has clinical value. It spares the practising analyst fruitless concern about the historical truth of the memories and phantasies that arise in an analysis. Sandler thus makes a contribution, peripherally, to the vexed subject of the reality of memories of childhood sexual abuse. However, it is important to recognize that Sandler's concept of repression belongs to clinical theory and not to the metapsychological theory as described by Freud (1915d, 1915e). The fact remains that an explanation of details of neurotic symptomatology, masturbatory phantasies, and repetitive behaviours is impossible, unless it is assumed that they had precursors in real events and wish phantasies of early childhood, which succumbed to primal repression. Such an assumption follows from the content of dreams, transferences, and screen memories (see Chapter 2).

In what follows (Chapters 7, 8, and 9) an attempt has been made to distinguish, as far as possible, between observable phenomena (clinical facts) as they appear in abnormal mental states and the various explanatory concepts and theories that have been devised to account for them. Thus a comparison is made between Freud's theories as described in Chapters 1 and 2 and those introduced later by Klein, Fairbairn, and Kohut. As Chapter 8 will illustrate, narcissism is an example of a concept, like splitting, where the failure to distinguish between descriptive and explanatory usages has led to much confusion.

CHAPTER SEVEN

Psychoses
and psychoanalytic theories
of development

From Freud onwards psychoanalytic theories of development depend on the premise that the manifestations of abnormal mental states reveal modes of mental activity more appropriate to the infant and young child. This assumption has a distinguished lineage in clinical neurology (Hughlings Jackson, see Chapter 1). Disinterest, inattention, and self-neglect characteristic of established cases of schizophrenia led Abraham (1908) and Freud (1911c) to postulate that, in this loss of the capacity for object love (object libidinal cathexis), there could be discerned evidence of the auto-erotism of the infant—a stage of the libido preceding object choice. An intermediate stage of narcissism was then proposed occurring between auto-erotism and object love on the basis of the phenomena characteristic of persecutory paranoia (Freud, 1911c). In these cases (paranoid psychosis, paranoid schizophrenia) the persecutor is known, is of the same sex, and was previously admired. Freud (1911c) hypothesized that this object choice is narcissistic. It occurs either because the libido has failed to pass beyond the stage of narcissism in the course of development or because the inability to maintain object love (object libidinal cathexis) leads to a libidinal regression to fixations established at the narcissistic stage.

The belief that psychotic symptoms hold the key to an understanding of early childhood mental development is exemplified by Abraham's paper on libidinal development in the light of mental disorders (*The Growth of Object Love*, Abraham, 1924). In this paper, Abraham compares obsessional neuroses with manic–depressive psychoses. The comparison rests on the many similarities between these conditions—the content of compulsive thoughts, the content of self-reproaches, and the obsessional practices that often accompany a depressive state. The outstanding difference between the two illnesses is that in obsessional neuroses a working transference appears, while this is absent when a manic–depression is at its height. Abraham (1924) interpreted this difference as due to the retention of the object in the former and its loss in the latter.

Abraham (1924) took as the starting-point for his investigation into the immediate cause of patients' manic–depression the periods of remission that occur between attacks. He observed that "the event which ushers in the actual melancholic illness" (Abraham, 1924) is object loss or the threat of object loss. Some of the phenomena found in his cases, he believed, could be attributed to introjection and identification with the lost love object. Noting that constipation and diarrhoea were commonplace, he concluded that his patients unconsciously identified the lost object with faeces. Constipation reflected a retention of the object, while diarrhoea represented its expulsion.

Returning to the comparison between obsessional neurosis and manic–depression, Abraham (1924) hypothesized that where object loss or the threat of object loss occurred, an immediate re-activation (through regression) of anal–sadistic tendencies took place in both illnesses. An obsessional neurosis appeared when the (psychical) destructive "acts" aimed at the object (identified with faeces) were halted and the object spared. A melancholic (manic–depressive) depression followed when ". . . sadistic anal-tendencies were victorious—those which aimed at destroying and expelling the object".

A number of clinical observations led Abraham (1924) to believe that introjecting the lost object occurred by way of the mouth.

Depressed patients exhibited what he described as "strong per-
verse cravings which consisted in using the mouth in the place of
the genitals" (Abraham, 1924). The patients also presented a variety of oral–sadistic phantasies—of biting and devouring the lost
object. Abraham (1924) supplemented this data with others drawn
from healthy persons in a state of mourning. In one instance an
oral–sadistic phantasy of the wish to restore the lost love object
by devouring the deceased's flesh was expressed. The depressed
patient thus introjected the lost object orally and then destroyed it
orally. These cannibalistic phantasies were, in Abraham's (1924)
opinion, responsible for the loss of appetite and refusal of food that
is so common in severe depressive states (food = flesh of the lost
object).

Abraham made another observation which he used to support
his theory of manic–depressive depression. He found, concomitantly with the cannibalistic phantasies, that his patients also ". . .
longed to use the mouth in a manner quite at variance with the
biting and eating phantasies" (Abraham, 1924). On the basis of the
hypothesis that the lost object was represented by faeces, the symptom of constipation could be seen as a reaction against an anal-
sadistic phantasy in which the introjected object is expelled anally
and destroyed. Faeces represented the murdered body of the lost
object. Thus in manic–depressive depressions the lost object is
introjected orally, attacked orally, and then murdered by anal
means. Loss of the object for the manic–depressive patient is
equivalent to psychical murder. In maniacal attacks a similar
process—introjection and expulsion of the object—occurs, but at
a rapid rate—hence the compulsive eating and psychomotor overactivity.

The proposition that the patient who suffers from an obsessional neurosis preserves and retains the object, while the
manic–depressive patient expels and destroys the object represented by faeces, led Abraham (1924) to theorize that these
different instinctual aims present in the two illnesses were representations of the libidinal aims belonging to two stages within
the anal–sadistic phase of libidinal development. He writes: ". . .
we find ourselves led to assume that stage includes two different
levels within itself. On the later level the conserving tendencies of
retaining and controlling the object, whereas on the earlier level

those hostile to the object—those of destroying and losing it come to the fore" (Abraham, 1924). An obsessional neurosis occurs when there is an instinctual regression to the level at which the object is retained. In manic–depressions the regression is to the earlier stage of anal–sadism with expulsion of the object. The periods of remission in manic–depressions follow when there is an advance from the earlier to the later stage of anal–sadism. The oral phenomena which Abraham (1924) observed in his depressed patients caused him to claim that the regression did not halt at the early stage of anal–sadism but continued on to the oral stage of the libido.

The presence of oral–sadistic phantasies and phantasies of pleasurable sucking in manic–depressions (he had observed the latter in a case of schizophrenia—Abraham, 1916), led Abraham to propose that two distinct oral sexual aims occurred in manic depressions. The first was to suck, the second to bite and destroy the object. Theorizing that these phenomena had infantile prototypes, Abraham proposed that during the oral stage of infantile libidinal development there were two distinct phases—one where sucking was the aim and a later one where the aim was to bite the object. The latter emerged with the eruption of the teeth. Similarly at the anal–sadistic stage there was an early phase in which the object was destroyed and a later one when it was preserved and controlled.

According to Abraham (1924), in obsessional neuroses and manic–depressions the object is degraded to faeces. Patients thus relate in different ways (retention, expulsion) to part of an object (partial object love). He supported this theory of the part object and partial object love with two sets of clinical observations. First, he discerned signs of partial object love in patients recovering from manic–depressions. This meant to Abraham (1924) that the aim of destroying the object, dominant at the time of the acute attack, had been replaced by a wish to preserve the object by only destroying a part of it. The remainder was spared. Second, he noted that in two cases of kleptomania there was "a peculiar and incomplete object love" (Abraham, 1924). They related to part of the love object only. The content of their phantasies was to bite off a part of the object and incorporate it. The mother was represented by her breast, the father by his penis. There was a regression from complete to partial object love.

Abraham (1924) found support for his concept of the part and partial incorporation in reports published by Staerke (1919) and van Ophuijsen (1920). They proposed that the persecutor in cases of paranoia is represented by the faecal mass in the anal canal. This was an extension of the observation (Ferenczi, 1912) that fear of anal penetration was present in cases of paranoia. The faecal mass in the anal canal represented the persecutor's penis (Staerke, 1919). In contrast to the depressive patient who incorporates and destroys the object, the paranoiac incorporates part of the object (Abraham, 1924). In terms of Abraham's theory of psychopathogenesis, the paranoiac regresses to the earlier of the two anal–sadistic phases and achieves incorporation of part of the object.

Abraham (1924) proceeded to include his concept of the part object into the schema of the growth of object love. At the beginning of infantile life there is a non-ambivalent sucking phase. This is succeeded by the oral and anal stages, when there are sadistic attacks on the object (the mother), as occurs in manic–depressions. As the infant proceeds to the second anal stage as in obsessional neuroses, the attacks are gradually modified. At first this modification results in part of the object being destroyed so that the remainder may be saved (the stage of partial object love). As development proceeds to the genital phase, attacks on the incorporated object lessen. Eventually the object is preserved in its entirety and valued (full object love). Such an evolution is interfered with if fixations occur at the stages of oral and anal sadism. This leads to the formation of a predisposition to obsessional neuroses and manic–depressions.

The developmental theories
of Klein and Fairbairn

Abraham's (1924) work has been presented in detail, for it bears heavily on the theories of Klein and Fairbairn. These writers, like Abraham (1924), attribute primary importance to the role of the mother in mental development, and to that extent the influence of the father is diminished. For the first time in psychoanalytic theorizing on development and mental pathology, hatred, destructiveness, and acquisitiveness are given greater prominence than the libido.

Abraham's concepts of oral incorporation, expulsion of the damaged or dangerous object (projection), oral sadism, the part object, and the protection of the incorporated object from destructive attacks play a prominent role in the developmental theories of Klein and Fairbairn. The part object (the breast) becomes the first object representation, in contrast to Abraham (1924), who held it to be a sacrifice to protect and conserve the object. Fairbairn excludes faeces as a part object, regarding the breast and penis only as natural objects. This is in accord with the anti-instinctual bias of his theory. Following Abraham, the incorporated object, part object for Klein and Fairbairn, has to be protected. Klein (1932, 1946) thinks of these attacks as instinctual (oral, anal, and urethral sadism), taking the form of unconscious phantasies. Fairbairn (1944) (see Chapter 10) regards the attacks on the object (part or whole) as emanating from endopsychic structures—the anti-libidinal ego and the rejecting object. Klein and Fairbairn extend the protection to the ego, which is believed to be in danger of fragmenting. Appropriate defences are described (Fairbairn, 1944; Klein, 1946). Introjected (incorporated) objects that, are damaged or dangerous are expelled and then re-introjected as Abraham postulated. The psychical (anal) expulsion is expressed as an unconscious phantasy (projective identification) in the Kleinian theory. Fairbairn holds the expulsion to be in the nature of a special technique (Fairbairn, 1944)—a paranoid technique that expels the "bad" objects/faeces.

The theory that psychotic phenomena reveal supposed characteristics of infantile mental processes played a part in the decision by Fairbairn and Klein to use psychiatric nomenclature to describe these processes. Fairbairn's (1940, 1944) experiences of patients, classified by him as schizoid because their overvaluation of phantasy at the expense of reality, their latent or overt omnipotence, and their separating thought from affect led him to postulate that a similar schizoid splitting (see Chapter 6) exists in earliest infancy. The aim is to suck (Abraham's oral phase one: preambivalent) rather than to bite (Abraham's phase two: oral sadism). This schizoid position will grow to dominate subsequent development if the infant comes to regard his love as bad and destructive. If it be so perceived due to oral disappointments, then there will be an increasing movement towards phantasy and the neglect of reality (Fairbairn, 1944). From his observations on depressed patients where the conflict is over greed and hate, Fairbairn (1944) postulated an infantile depressive position occurring at Abraham's second oral stage (oral sadism). Whether or not this depressive position will gain an ascendancy depends on the extent to which the individual's mothering is satisfying or frustrating.

Klein (1932, 1935, 1940, 1946) made more use of psychiatric nomenclature to underscore her conviction of the similarities that exist between the anxieties of the infant and those of the adolescent or adult psychotic patient (psychotic anxieties). Like Fairbairn, Klein's preference for the concept of infantile positions follows from the hypothesis that the psychical constituents of these positions—the unconscious (omnipotent) phantasies and the resulting psychotic anxieties—persist throughout life in varying degrees of intensity. The term paranoid–schizoid describes a psychical situation akin to that which exists in a patient suffering from a persecutory type of psychosis (paranoid schizophrenia, paranoid psychosis). Normally the infantile psychotic (persecutory) anxieties, arising from the threat to the introjected part object, do not predominate, but when they do a predisposition is formed for the later development of a persecutory type of psychosis. As for later development, Klein (1940) postulates a depressive position and a manic defence. Her description of the manic defence is recognized in that small group of patients where a manic attack follows real object loss. In the manic attack the lost object is restored or brought back to life. Klein attributes to the infant the omnipotence of these particular manic patients who deny their murderous act and make reparation.

The data (the clinical facts) that are used to support the theory that adult psychoses can provide information about the processes involved in mental development are not simply observational. They also consist of the interpretations of the selfsame phenomena. Oral sadistic phantasies and oral incorporation of the object are not invariable manifestations of manic–depressive states. They may appear directly in some cases—particularly where real object loss has occurred—but their absence is also common especially when there is no evidence of real loss or a real threat of object loss

(Bibring, 1953). In severe and moderately severe depressive states precipitated by events other than object loss, the self-reproaches may be seen as the result of hatred that cannot find an outlet other than against the self. There is no real evidence that this hatred is directed against an internalized object. A case of this type follows.

A man aged 45 had suffered from three moderately severe attacks of manic–depressive depression—the first at 18 years, when he went to university in his home town. He was married, with three children. He was in analytic treatment for 4 years, leading to an improvement in his mental state. During the analysis there were periods when he was retarded in thought and action. At these times the transference relationship that had been established vanished from sight, only to reappear as the retardation lifted. During the analysis he never complained of gastro-intestinal symptoms. Neither did he become aware of oral-sadistic phantasies. He was very self-critical. Many of his utterances could have been interpreted in terms of oral sadism—for example, his complaint that he was over-demanding of his wife and the author. Real object loss or the threat of real object loss played no part in the precipitation of the attacks. There was dread of the loss of love when faced with an inability to reach his unrealistic ego-ideals. This demand upon himself led to frustration and anger, which was ultimately self-directed.

It may be that cases of this kind led Abraham in 1915, nine years before his 1924 paper, to write to Freud as follows: ". . . the postulation in your short manuscript that the reproaches directed against the melancholic's own ego are really directed against another person, I am not yet convinced of this, and I do not remember your bringing detailed proof in your paper" (Abraham, 1915). Was Abraham justified in dispelling these doubts, as he did in the 1924 paper?

It may be said that the self-reproaches of the depressed patient provide the model for Klein's (1940) concept of the depressive position. The mother is now perceived as a whole object instead of simply a breast (part object). Having lost the mother at weaning, the infant attributes this loss to the injury he has inflicted on her through his envy and greed. These are the depressive anxieties. These anxieties may be mild or severe, depending on the intensity of the psychical attacks made on the breast. It is their persistence in such forms that contributes to the predisposition to depressive illness in later life. Klein (1940) writes, "This is the state of mind in the baby which I termed the depressive position and I suggested it is a melancholia 'in statu nascendi'. The object being mourned is the mother's breast. . . . " With the appearance of the depressive position, a series of defences (denial, omnipotence, reparation) are evoked to soften the impact of the loss and to restore the physical integrity of the mother. This is the manic defence to which reference was made. In this theory of the depressive position Klein follows Abraham (1924), who identified real or psychical object loss as the immediate cause of severe depressive illness and thus as a pathological form of mourning. Object loss (weaning) became the significant event ushering in the depressive position (Klein, 1935, 1940). However, in relying on the symptoms of adult depressions as the building blocks of her developmental theory, she was not mindful of the fact that these illnesses are not necessarily precipitated by real object loss.

The content of schizophrenic delusions consists more often of sexual ideas of a pleasurable or distressing nature than of oral–sadistic phantasies. Even when these are delusions with an oral–sadistic content it is possible to observe an underlying sexual (masturbatory) conflict. For example, a male schizophrenic patient demanded that a canine tooth be extracted because he could not stop touching it with his tongue. Extracted, the tooth would no longer be a means of experiencing an unwanted pleasurable sensation (Freeman, 1973). Similarly, the destructive content of schizophrenic delusions that are offered as support for the role of aggression in mental development frequently screen erotic phantasies (Bleuler, 1911).

The mixture of clinical facts and interpretations of the same, which provide the basis for developmental theories, is to be found in the case of transitivistic phenomena that arise in the course of a (schizophrenic) patient–analyst interaction. These are interpreted as resulting from introjection and projection of parts of the self and objects (Rosenfeld, 1954). These interrelations are thought to reflect infantile mental processes. However, the absence of transitivistic signs does not prevent other phenomena being interpreted as evidence of self–object confusion. Thus schizoid mechanisms—splitting and projective identification—are held to be responsible for inattention, withdrawal, and negativism. Interpretation brings into line disparate phenomena and gives a consistency to the explanatory concepts. In this way, the great variation that characterizes the symptomatology of the schizophrenias, for example, may be ignored. This variability which is also present in the courses that psychoses follow, weakens the theory that psychotic phenomena present psychical situations analogous to those that occur in the healthy child.

The psychoanalyst does not stray far from what is observed when he identifies mental conflict in the content of delusions and hallucinations. Wish phantasies of all kinds clash with fear of retribution. He is still close to the clinical facts when he interprets the delusional and hallucinatory content as the externalization and projection of unwanted wish phantasies. There is no certainty, in the individual case, of knowing whether or not the psychotic conflict exists in an identical form prior to the onset of the psychosis. Sometimes this is possible when a patient continues psychotherapy after the remission of an attack. When a relapse occurs, the conflict as expressed in the content of delusions is identical to that discerned in the patient prior to the attack.

Do Klein or Fairbairn's theories do justice to the complex unconscious mental processes that occur in psychoses by explaining them in terms of unconscious (infantile) phantasies that have been exposed by the morbid process? The problem may be illustrated by the following case:

A 15-year-old girl fell ill with a schizophrenic psychosis. There was a protracted pre-psychotic phase. The first psychotic symptom was her complaint that a boy she knew was watching her through a telescope while she bathed. When the illness reached its acute stage with persecutory ideas of different kinds, she was forever admiring her naked body in the mirror, touching her breasts and buttocks with pleasure and pride.

Following the Klein theory of psychopathogenesis, the delusion of being observed would be attributed to her "looking self", symbolized by the telescope, being split off from the ego and forcibly projected into the boy (an unconscious phantasy). The acute attack that followed might be interpreted as the expression of a manic defence (omnipotence, denial of psychical reality) whose aim was to deny, psychically, the reality of the persecution.

There is another explanation, which looks to the changes that affected the mental derivatives of instinct and consequently the nature of the patient's object relations. These changes are not necessarily connected with the psychical events of early childhood (Katan, 1979). The course that the illness followed suggests that the active sexual aim of looking (scoptophilia) had changed during the period of the delusion of observation and prior to the full development of the psychosis. In that acute stage there was no longer any sign of the delusion of being looked at. She looked at herself. At the onset of the psychosis, it may be hypothesized, she had renounced the wish to look at a sexual object (the boy). This renunciation could not occur through repression, because that function had already been damaged by the partial dissolution of the self. A more elementary defence came into operation. The wish to look had turned back on her own self (Freud, 1915c). An alternative sexual aim emerged as a result—the wish to be looked at (exhibitionism). A new subject was introduced (the boy with the telescope substituted for the "looking self"). She now unconsciously displayed herself at bath times, so that her wish phantasy of being looked at was fulfilled. This may be thought of as an attempt at recovery—to regain the world of objects lost with the dissolution (Freud, 1911c). With the increasing dissolution of self occurring in the acute attack, the scoptophilic instinct turned back on self (looking at the naked body in the mirror). It may be said, following Freud (1915c), that the original auto-erotic nature of scoptophilia was reinstated.

Before concluding this chapter, it is important to turn again to the concept of the part-object, which is used exclusively by Klein and Fairbairn in their theories of psychopathogenesis and mental development. Its basis in clinical observation is questionable. Abraham (1924) as has already been described, preferred to interpret phantasies about the penis, breast, and faeces as literally parts of the object. These parts were expendable. Thus the remainder of the object was left intact. He apparently rejected the alternative explanation of these mental contents—namely that they are the expression of an early form of abstract thinking—the *"pars pro toto"*. This means of representation is commonly encountered in dreams, in the thinking of schizophrenic patients (see Chapter 1), and in common parlance. Ambivalence leads to a person being described as a "shit"; a symbol for the breast stands for a woman. Abraham's (1924) reliance on Staerke's (1919) and van Ophuijsen's (1920) theories may be criticized along the same lines. These writers were content to assume that the faecal mass in the anal canal (a part object) represented the persecutor's penis in cases of paranoia. This theory, as a reading of the original papers portrays, was based solely on the utterances of a few psychotic patients and on the dreams of neurotic patients. The content of the dreams of the neurotic patient consisted of being attacked by men or dogs. The psychotic patients hinted at the fear of being penetrated anally by the persecutor (Ferenczi, 1912). The concept of a persecuting (i.e. bad) part-object—an idea taken up by both Klein and Fairbairn—is based on interpretation of the clinical phenomena. The concept (the part-object) is no less theoretical than that of splitting (see Chapter 6). It is now part of theories of mental development (Klein, 1935; Fairbairn, 1944) as the first form of object representation.

CHAPTER EIGHT

Theories of narcissistic object relations

The concept of narcissism is used in both a descriptive and an explanatory sense. It describes the tendency to over-value and idealize mental and physical aspects of the self and objects (Freud, 1914c). An individual may overvalue his body, powers of thought, judgement, ideals, and ethical standards. The lover idealizes his beloved, and the homosexual man overvalues his partner's body, and the penis in particular. The concept of narcissism is also used to explain certain characteristics of a relationship that exists between one individual and another. The psychoanalytic treatment of male homosexuals led to the hypothesis that the love object of the male homosexual represents his own self (ego), either as he is, as he once was, or as he wishes to be (Freud, 1914c). The homosexual love object is based on the wish to recover the adolescent or childhood self while the individual plays the part of the mother. Again the choice may spring from the wish to possess a virile body. These types of object choice are described as narcissistic because of the involvement of the self. Such (narcissistic) choice may also be inferred from the characteristics of the object choice of heterosexual men and women.

The usage of the terms narcissism and narcissistic is further complicated by the fact that the concept is an integral part of the libido theory. Freud (1916–17) confined the concept of libido to the "instinctual forces of sexual life", thus emphasizing its qualitative and quantitative characteristics. Narcissism describes the hypothetical "quantities" of libido (cathexes) that exist within the self. Primary narcissism is the reservoir of libido present at the beginning of life. From then there is a gradual movement of libidinal cathexes from the rudimentary self to objects. When identification with these objects takes place, there is a return to the self of the libidinal cathexes that were invested in these objects (secondary narcissism). When the libido is optimally distributed between the self and object, the ego libido (secondary narcissism) provides the basis for a balanced sense of self-esteem. This normal or healthy narcissism is quite different from the manifestations brought together under the concept of pathological narcissism.

When clinical phenomena are conceptualized in accordance with the theory of the distribution and redistribution of libidinal cathexes, it is important to note that in such a formulation the concept of narcissism is used in a manner different to the explanatory usage of the term. To illustrate this, there is the example of the withdrawal, disinterest, and inattention that is present in long-standing cases of hebephrenic–catatonic schizophrenia. These phenomena may be interpreted as resulting from detachment of libidinal cathexes from object representations and their return to the self. This theoretical use of the term narcissistic is to be distinguished from the way it is employed and understood in the case of other clinical phenomena that appear in these psychoses, delusional phantasies, and transitivism (Bleuler, 1911). Here the term "narcissistic" is used to describe narcissistic object relations.

The boundary of the self
and narcissistic object relations

I

A fundamental component of the theory of narcissistic object relations is the concept of the boundary of the self—that boundary which differentiates the self representations from object representations. The process of object choice that occurs in male homosexuals provides a prototype for narcissistic object choice in general. It reveals the potential permeability of that boundary which exists between self and object representations. In male homosexuals wished-for aspects of the self are unconsciously perceived in the love object. This leads to a merging of self and object. The sexual practices of these individuals and their partners—the reversal of roles and sexual aims, active to passive and vice versa—indicates that what has been externalized can be easily returned to the self. The permeability of the boundary of the self is at its height under the impact of sexual need. Self and object are interchangeable until the need is satisfied, when the boundary regains much, if not all, of its integrity.

The hypothesis that the boundary delineating the self from object representation is potentially permeable is also founded on transference phenomena that appear during the analysis of patients with symptom and character neuroses (Nunberg, 1955). Here there is an overvaluation of the analyst. The analyst has become the repository of an idealized self (Kohut, 1971). This attribution of omnipotence and omniscience inevitably leads to an unwillingness to accept the realities of the analytic process and of the analyst (A. Freud, 1954). When there is disparagement of the analyst, he has become endowed with aspects of the patient's self, past or present, that were or are unacceptable to him.

In the functional psychoses and organic mental states the boundary between the self and object representations is so seriously disrupted that the patient can no longer distinguish his own sensations, percepts, ideas, wishes, and fears from those of others. What can be inferred about the alteration to the boundary of the self in non-psychotic individuals may be directly observed in this phenomenon of transitivism. At the acute onset of schizophrenic psychoses patients attribute aspects of their mental and physical selves to others and perceive aspects of others in themselves. A persecutor is held responsible for what is experienced. Apart from sexual excitement, wish phantasies and thoughts, speech ("He is cursing me with my voice"), and memories are perceived in the persecutor (Freeman, 1964). The patient feels part or all of the persecutor's body within the boundaries of his own physical self (Freeman, 1962a).

II

Klein's (1946) theory of narcissism is predicated on the boundary concept. The boundary may be crossed in either direction, so that elements of the self pass into objects and parts of the object into the self. The narcissistic phenomena of the psychoses, and the inferences drawn from psychoanalytic work with children and adults (non-psychotic), led Klein (1946) to postulate that these psychical movements require a prior splitting of the self and object (See Chapter 6). Thus splitting provides the precondition for the expulsion of parts of the self into objects (projective identification) and for the incorporation of parts of the object into the self (introjection). Narcissism, in the sense of its consisting of a psychical state where all or part of the self exists within an object, springs from the action of schizoid mechanisms (splitting and projective identification). Here narcissistic object relations are the result of the heightened action of mental mechanisms that are part of healthy mental development.

Klein's theory of narcissism seemed most relevant to the narcissistic object relations characteristic of the schizophrenias and paranoid psychoses. The schizophrenic patient's sensitivity or apparent lack of it could now be regarded as resulting from the action of schizoid mechanisms, rather than resulting from a libidinal decathexis of object representations and a return of the libido to the self. Rosenfeld (1950, 1952, 1954) held that the positive and negative autistic phenomena with which he was confronted were the expression of unconscious phantasies in which he, as object, had become immediately involved. The clinical phenomena thus followed from an endopsychic object relationship in which the patient's self was split into fragments and expelled into Rosenfeld (1952, 1954). The cause of the withdrawal, inattention, and negativism was the patient's perception of Rosenfeld as a cruel and terrifying figure. He became so because he was now the repository of the patient's acquisitive and sadistic phantasies. The transitivistic phenomena resulted from projective identification.

As a result of merging, the object (Rosenfeld) no longer existed as a separate entity and so could not be the focus of sadism springing from envy (Rosenfeld, 1987).

To describe the causal relationship between the pathologically exaggerated schizoid mechanisms and the autistic phenomena characteristic of the schizophrenias, Rosenfeld (1964) coined the term "omnipotent narcissistic object relations". This emphasized the omnipotent nature of the psychical processes involved (the schizoid mechanisms). These processes enabled the patient to dispense with his envy and greed not only through their expulsion into objects, but also by splitting the object into "good" and "bad". The former was idealized. Through splitting, the "good" object was spared sadistic attacks. The "bad" object now represented, through projection, the patient's sadistic acquisitiveness. It was thus possible for the patient to believe that he still possessed the "good" object and its qualities. The greater the degree of envy, the greater the need for omnipotent narcissistic object relations. If these relationships, based on schizoid mechanisms, weaken, envy returns in full force, as the object is now perceived as separate from the self.

Working with patients with character disorders, Rosenfeld (1964, 1971, 1987) was impressed by their narcissistic attitudes. They had difficulty in forming and sustaining satisfying relationships. They were extremely egocentric and indifferent to others. This indifference could easily extend to the self. At the same time Rosenfeld (1971), like Fairbairn (1940), discerned an omnipotence that was hidden or expressed in idealizations of one sort or another. The analytic work revealed that they were intensely envious, but, as with the omnipotence and hate, this was far from consciousness. The repetition in the transference of the narcissistic manifestations not infrequently led to a negative therapeutic reaction. These patients projected their envy into figures outside the analysis, so that Rosenfeld could remain a "good" object. It seemed to him that the narcissistic object relations of these patients had much in common with those found in the schizophrenias. They had a common source—schizoid mechanisms. The narcissism of the psychotic and non-psychotic patients was destructive rather than libidinal (Rosenfeld, 1971). Unbeknown to the patient, this destructive narcissism was idealized. It afforded a source of pleasure and protection. Every object libidinal wish had to be destroyed. The non-psychotic patients had a compulsive need to be in psychoanalytic treatment so that they could have an object, in the person of the analyst, to attack and destroy (Rosenfeld, 1987).

To explain why these patients had this relentless need to undermine, damage, and destroy everything that was good in the self and others, Rosenfeld (1971, 1987) reverted to the theory of the death instinct. He did so because his patients produced a plethora of phantasies and dreams that had a murderous content. The more the patients tried to work co-operatively and constructively in the analysis, the more intense and frightening these dreams and phantasies became. Only the death instinct, Rosenfeld (1987) believed, could have the power to produce such manifestations. In these cases he held that the death instinct had not fused with the life instinct, leaving it free to drive the individual to psychical death.

Rosenfeld's theory of a destructive narcissism has common ground with Freud's libidinal narcissism. Both point to the characteristic overvaluation of specific content of thought, conscious and unconscious. For Rosenfeld, the overvaluation is of elements of the self that have particular malignancy. These elements come together to form destructive narcissistic organizations, which the remainder of the self has to placate. These psychical organizations, derived from the death instinct, are active in the psychoses, where their effects are much clearer to see. The schizoid mechanisms of splitting and projective identification are constantly at work to prevent psychical annihilation.

Kohut's theory of narcissistic object relations

Kohut's (1971) theory of the development of narcissism is based on psychoanalytic work with patients whose condition he described as "narcissistic personality disorders". These patients complained of low self-esteem, of being inhibited in interpersonal relationships, and of a feeling of inferiority. Symptoms of anxiety and depression of mood were commonplace. They had much in common with those described by Fairbairn (1940) as schizoid.

As analysis proceeded, Kohut observed the hallmarks of narcissistic object relations—idealization, overvaluation, omnipotence, and a blurring of the boundary between self and object. The patients overvalued Kohut, believing him to be omnipotent. They adopted or attempted to adopt what they imagined were his values and ideals. Some patients did not seem to perceive Kohut as separate from themselves. The patient believed that Kohut was a replica—a mirror image of himself. There were those whose only interest in Kohut, recognized as a separate individual, was as a means of immediately satisfying an emotional need. Kohut (1971) described these forms of relating as "idealizing" and "mirror" transferences. The patients were relating to him as a self-object (Kohut, 1971).

As long as the idealizing and mirror transferences were not disturbed, the patient felt content and secure. Loss of these transferences, through dissatisfaction with Kohut's behaviour and responses or from the inevitable interruptions in the routine of the analysis, led to anger, despondency, criticism of Kohut, self-reproach, and a return to the state of mind that had preceded the analysis. Kohut (1971) concluded that he was observing the results of a faulty development of narcissism. The unrestricted narcissism of infancy and early childhood had persisted, and, though hidden from view for the most part, now found direct expression in the relationship with Kohut.

The idealizing and mirror transferences were the different ways in which the libido presented itself. The former was the expression of an idealized parental imago, while the latter was the expression of a grandiose self. The power of these psychical constellations and their distinctness from one another led Kohut (1971) to hypothesize that they were separate forms of libido. He proposed that the narcissistic disorders presented early infantile stages of ego and object libido. Each form of the libido had its own line of development. When the libidinal constellations (idealized parental imago and grandiose self) are transformed in the course of development, self–object differentiation is optimally achieved; other persons are perceived realistically and an adequate form of self-esteem regulation is established. Faulty development occurs when the parents are unempathic and fail to meet the child's emotional needs. The conditions are then established for the persistence of the idealizing parental imago, the grandiose self, and self-object images for narcissistic object relations.

Kohut's (1971) theory breaks with Freud's (1914c) concept of a unitary libido, which evolves along the line: auto-erotism, narcissism, object love. This has tended, in Kohut's opinion, to encourage the belief that narcissism has an essentially pathological quality and must be overcome and replaced by object love if healthy mental life is to be achieved. Kohut's concepts of "ego" and "object libido" are part of his theory of the self and its development (Kohut, 1977). The self will only become resilient and stable and develop a "healthy self-assertiveness" (Kohut, 1977) through "transmuting internalizations". These internalizations, dependent on parental empathy and responsiveness, are essential for the transformation of the infantile libidinal constellations (self-objects, etc.). Without transmuting internalizations, the basic structures of the self are deprived of the cathexes necessary for their healthy evolution.

Narcissistic object relations
as the outcome of defence

Kohut's theory that narcissistic object relations arise from an anomalous development of ego and object libido was a departure from Freud's (1914c) theory that these abnormal forms of relating follow from a pathological narcissism—i.e., an enhanced ego libido at the expense of object libido. Kohut's (1971) psychopathology of narcissism dispenses with the theory that pathological narcissism represents a defence against anxieties caused by phantasies and affects.

The theory that narcissistic object relations are the outcome of a defence is common to those who subscribe to Freud's libido theory and to those who follow Klein's (1946) theory of schizoid mechanisms. The origin of the concept of a defensive (pathological) narcissism (Abraham, 1919; Balint, 1935; Glover, 1949; Nunberg, 1955) may be traced to the treatment of non-psychotic patients clinically similar to those treated by Fairbairn (1940), Kohut (1971), and Rosenfeld (1987). There is the difficulty in initiating and sustaining a therapeutic process. There is evidence of omnipotence and of the phenomena that indicate that the self–object barrier is permeable. There is a fluidity in the patient–analyst situation. In the course of treatment the patients switch roles with the analyst.

In one case, for example, the slightest sign of what the patient interpreted as a withdrawal of interest on the author's part— change of time of the session, slight delay in starting, meeting another patient by accident—led to resistance. This took the form of an aggressive silence. It was punctuated by verbal criticisms. On one occasion the patient began to describe an incident pertaining to the analysis. Then he forgot what he was going to say. However, he continued that a friend had been about to confide in him and then changed his mind. The patient was distressed by this. He was identifying himself with the frustrating friend. He thus reversed roles and disappointed the author, hoping he would annoy him as the friend had done. In disappointing the author, he was giving expression to the disappointment he had experienced in the past. He deprived the author of "material", just as his mother has deprived him of love and attention.

The omnipotent phantasies that narcissistic patients exhibit are a means of reversing a sense of helplessness, hopelessness, and frustration. This is most obvious in the case of the wish delusions of long-standing cases of schizophrenia (see Chapter 1).

A non-psychotic male patient suffered from anxiety attacks during analytical sessions. These, it transpired, were caused by phantasies of being attacked and anally penetrated with an instrument that the author kept hidden. In his masturbatory phantasies he omnipotently controlled his victim, perpetrating sadistic acts, including penetrating the anus with an instrument (as a child he was repeatedly subject to enemata because of obdurate constipation). He recalled that in childhood masturbation he personified his penis, which he then subjected to every command. The sensation of power he experienced in his phantasies was the counterpart and reaction to the sense of helplessness he felt *vis-à-vis* the author.

These clinical phenomena may be interpreted in terms of the libido theory. Object libido is converted into ego (narcissistic) libido following the internalization and identification with the objects who were the cause of the patient's helplessness, disappointment, and frustration. Passivity was changed into activity, thus providing a potent defence. A pathological narcissism was established, leading to narcissistic object relations. This narcissism followed the model of secondary narcissism where there is differentiation between self and object images.

The phenomena described above may be conceptualized in terms of Klein's (1946) theory of narcissistic object relations. That they are the outcome of a defence is inherent in the theory. The aim of the defence is to preserve the self and the "good" object (analyst), with which it is identified, from the damaging impact of the death instinct as represented by the overvalued destructive elements of the self with their envy and sadism (Rosenfeld's "destructive narcissism"). Steiner (1993) introduced the concept of "pathological organizations" of the personality to denote the psychical processes (schizoid mechanisms) that act to defend against the anxiety posed by the destructiveness of the psychical representations of the death instinct. The destructive elements within the self may be contained by their projection into objects selected for their potential to injure and destroy. When the pathological organizations succeed in their defensive role, they provide what Steiner (1993) calls a "retreat". This retreat not only ensures a relief from the intolerable anxiety posed by threat of fragmentation of the self, but it also offers a means and opportunity for the free expression of (omnipotent) phantasy.

Narcissistic object relations and pathological narcissism

The concepts of narcissistic object relations and pathological narcissism differ in one particular and important respect. With the exception of the psychoses, the former describes clinical phenomena from which the inference is drawn that self and object representations are not clearly differentiated. The latter is theoretical. It is based on the libido theory and provides a hypothetical account of the way in which unconscious mental events (redistribution of libidinal cathexes from object to self) lead to the phenomena collectively described as "narcissistic object relations". This theory is rejected by Klein and Kohut. Klein's (1946) view is that narcissistic object relations are founded on self–object relations governed by schizoid mechanisms. Rosenfeld (1987) goes further with his theory of destructive narcissism. Kohut (1971, 1977) understands narcissistic object relations as resulting from deficiencies in the development of the self. In these theories there seems to be no place for the concept of pathological narcissism.

While allowing for the differences in form that exist between non-psychotic and psychotic patients, their attitudes and manner of relating may be described as narcissistic. There are psychotic states whose manner of relating, at the onset of the illness, bears the closest resemblance to that which is present in non-psychotic disorders. These similarities disappear as the psychotic process pursues its course. A striking example of this similarity and eventual dissimilarity is the transference love that may manifest itself in some character disorders. It also occurs in the erotomania that precedes the appearance of persecutory delusions and hallucinations (Freeman, 1984). The non-psychotic patient idealizes the analyst as the psychotic patient overvalues her imagined lover. In both categories sufficient data is forthcoming to indicate that analyst and beloved are narcissistic object choices. When the expectation of love from the idealized object is not forthcoming, a dramatic reaction follows. This can be observed at first hand in the case of the patient who is in analysis. There is an intensification of resistance, and this may lead to the treatment being abandoned. The patient is filled with hate. Something similar must be imagined in the case of the psychotic patient who has now come to regard her beloved as a persecutor. At this stage of the illness transitivistic phenomena are prominent. As far as content is concerned, it would appear they follow from an externalization of affects, phantasies, and cognitive processes (Freeman, 1964).

Sexuality, in all its forms, is at the centre of the theoretical concept of pathological narcissism. The homosexual male reveals

the sexual nucleus of his narcissism in the content of his masturbatory phantasies and in his sexual aims, whose object is the self.
This is not immediately obvious in the case of narcissistic and
schizoid personality disorders. However, where analytic treatment
takes place, it may become manifest. This was so in the patient
with the sadistic masturbatory phantasies (see above). The pathological narcissism (libidinal hypercathexis of the self) hypothesized to account for the narcissistic object relations provides a
defence against mental "pain" (helplessness, etc.)

The pathological narcissism envisaged as present in the psychoses deviates qualitatively from that of the pre-psychotic phase
of the illness. This is so because different psychical conditions
have established themselves following the dissolution of self–
object boundaries. While the pre-psychotic phase continues, these
boundaries were no more or less permeable than those of patients
suffering from narcissistic or schizoid personality disorders
(Katan, 1954). The pre-psychotic symptomatology is the outcome
of a defence following the model of secondary narcissism (Katan,
1979). It may be proposed that the dissolution of psychical structures (ego, etc.) exposes a primitive (psychotic) form of narcissism
(Ey, 1969; Jackson, 1884). It is comparable to the hypothetical primary narcissism and is thus distinct from the narcissism of the
pre-psychotic phase. It is expressed in the primary process which
is now in the ascendancy. The conflict of the pre-psychotic phase
that leads to the defence is now managed in a different manner.
Substitutions (object for self) are affected through displacement. In
the case of the psychotic woman here described, her sexuality,
which had the self as object, was embodied in her persecutor. The
conflict expressed in the erotomania was now dealt with through a
reconstruction of the self and object undertaken by the primary
process (Katan, 1979). The sexual and primitive nature of psychotic
narcissism is most clearly demonstrated in long-standing cases of
schizophrenia (Freeman, 1970). The masturbatory phantasies show
that the objects of the phantasies are representations of the self as
signs of narcissistic supremacy (Freeman, 1962b; Katan, 1954).

Theories of narcissistic object relations

There are three distinct theories of narcissistic object relations. There is the theory of pathological narcissism based on the libido theory (Freud, 1914c), the theory of schizoid mechanisms (Klein, 1946), and the theory of an abnormal development of narcissistic and object libido (Kohut, 1971). Common to both the Kleinian and Kohutian theories is the hypothesis that a unitary psychopathological process is responsible for the narcissistic object relations of both psychotic and non-psychotic patients. The fact that the narcissistic object relations of the former differ in form from those of the latter is attributed to the extent and intensity of the psychopathological process.

The Kleinian theory postulates psychical movement between positions (paranoid–schizoid, depressive). It underpins the hypothesis that in narcissistic and schizoid personality states the ego is buttressed by a manic defence (idealization, omnipotence, reparation) alongside the schizoid mechanisms appropriate to the paranoid–schizoid position. In the psychotic patient (the schizophrenias, etc.) the ego and its "good" objects are in danger of psychical annihilation from the derivatives of the death instinct. The manic defence is ineffective, and so to ward off the danger splitting and projective identification form defence organizations (Rosenfeld, 1987; Steiner, 1993). Thus the narcissistic object relations of both psychotic and non-psychotic patients follow from the operation of schizoid mechanisms.

In acknowledging the formal differences that exist between neurotic and psychotic illnesses, Kohut (1971) sees these differences as resulting from a single psychopathological process—namely, its effect on the idealized parental imago and the grandiose self. The outcome—narcissistic personality disorder or psychosis—is the consequence of these psychical "structures" being insufficiently modified (lacking "transmuting internalizations"), or of their being characterized by a brittleness caused by environmental and hereditary influences (Kohut, 1971). This leads to a fragmentation of the self and to the narcissistic object relations characteristic of psychoses.

The theory of pathological narcissism has its basis in the libido theory, and sexuality is at its core. In this regard it differs from the theories of Klein and Kohut, which are predominantly object-relation-centred. Klein's emphasis is on the role of the death instinct and its expression in destructiveness. According to the theory of pathological narcissism, the narcissistic object relations of non-psychotic and psychotic patients spring from different forms of narcissism—the one a pathological variant of secondary narcissism, the other a variant of primary narcissism (psychotic narcissism). A change in the nature of the pathological (secondary) narcissism takes place when there is extensive psychical dissolution. This event results in the exposure of an "undifferentiated state" (Katan, 1979). This disrupts the continuity between past and present and their psychical representations. The theory of pathological narcissism is incompatible with the concept of a psychopathological continuity between psychotic and non-psychotic disorders. Clinical experience supports this. In narcissistic and schizoid personality disorders transient failures of reality testing occur, resulting in brief delusional and hallucinatory phenomena. There is rarely movement to an established psychotic state (Kohut, 1971). Attempts to treat established cases of schizophrenia and paranoid psychoses, not simply acute psychotic attacks where remission is commonplace, show that the narcissistic object relations occurring in these conditions cannot be radically altered. The theories described here to account for narcissistic object relations reflect a long-standing controversy on the nature of non-psychotic and psychotic illness. Are they or are they not qualitatively distinct clinical entities?

CHAPTER NINE

On the formal aspects
of psychotic phenomena

C linical states treated by psychoanalysts do not necessarily require a special interest in the formal aspects of abnormal conscious mental events. The content of patients' utterances are the primary object of the analyst's attention. Patients' communications obey the rules of syntax, abstract thinking proceeds at an advanced level, and memory, although often subject to falsifications, is not impaired. The goal of thought is maintained, and extraneous stimuli do not disrupt the flow of associations. Interruptions may usually be resolved when the patient becomes aware, generally through the analyst's intervention, of an unwelcome preconscious wish, memory, or (transference) thought. Under these circumstances the dream acts as a reminder that there are mental phenomena whose formal characteristics are distinct from their content. In dreams the content is experienced as a "here-and-now" event. It has an hallucinatory quality.

Psychiatrists are familiar with those conscious abnormal events that are so strikingly different from the mental experiences of the healthy. In psychotic states, thinking, speech, perceiving, memory, and selective attention assume manifold and variegated forms.

Speech is impaired in its communicative function. This occurs when there is an obstruction (blocking) in the flow of speech; when there is a loss of thought connecting one theme with another (omissions); when the choice of words is determined by their sound rather than by their meaning; and when the stream of thought is "derailed" by the intrusion of external stimuli. Concepts lose their autonomy, leading to neologisms and paraphasias. There is "over-inclusive" thinking (Payne, 1961).

In the psychoses and organic mental states the perceptual modalities assume new forms with the loss of veridicality. Perception of real events is subject to misinterpretation, and there is perception of auditory, tactile, and visual events in the absence of the appropriate stimuli. The content of these illusions and hallucinations may be agreeable, distasteful, or frightening. As in dreams, the patient is locked into these experiences. The mental contents appear involuntarily. They occur alongside a mental self no longer sharply differentiated from that of others—hence the transitivistic phenomena (Bleuler, 1911). With the loss of awareness of the self as a distinct and autonomous entity (Federn, 1953), mental contents lose their locus of origin.

Reflecting on the characteristics of psychotic phenomena leads to many questions. How do phantasies become delusions? How does a repressed memory become changed into an auditory hallucination? What is the cause of the transitivistic phenomena? What is responsible for the loss of the communicative function of speech?

Theories that account for the form
of psychotic phenomena

As described in Chapter 8, theories accounting for the form of psychotic phenomena have centred around the hypothesis that these conscious pathological events give representations to modes of mental activity that might have had a place in the developmental process of the healthy child. The psychotic patient's certainty that his phantasies and abnormal perceptions are realities has its counterpart in early childhood, when conscious phantasy and reality are poorly differentiated. The loss of self–object discrimination may also be matched in early childhood. Faulty concept formation, as in the schizophrenias, is comparable to the kind of elementary abstraction observable in young children.

In early childhood affective ties with parents remain intact, despite the falsifications of reality relating to wishes and fears. These ties enable the child to acknowledge the limitations of his wish phantasies and to overcome the anxiety caused by frightening phantasies. Neither is possible in manic or schizophrenic psychoses, where object ties are either severed or lost.

In the psychoses disturbances in the form of thinking, perceiving, and remembering appear within the spheres of real and phantasy (delusional) object relations. This binding connection conceptualized in the (descriptive) concept of autism (Bleuler, 1911), between pathological forms of cognition and real object relations, is not valid for cases of chronic brain syndrome (arteriosclerotic dementia, Alzheimer's disease), as it is not for young children. Chronic brain syndrome differs from the psychoses in that whatever the manner of expression (misidentifications, etc.), the capacity to relate to others affectively, remains (Freeman, 1969).

The content of delusions and hallucinations signifies the presence of mental conflict. According to Arlow and Brenner (1969) and Pao (1979), the psychotic phenomena represent a compromise between unacceptable wish phantasies and defences appropriate to an ego that has been damaged by regression. The clinical phenomena thus have a defensive stamp. Their form depends on the manner in which the regressed ego and its defences give representation to the unconscious conflictual contents.

A contrary view is held by Katan (1954, 1979). He proposed that the ego no longer operates in that part of the mind affected by the psychotic process. The dissolution of psychical structure that attends the onset of the illness leads to the emergence of an "undifferentiated state". In this state ego is not differentiated from id. Self and object are no longer distinct from one another. The distinction between past and present is lost. This accounts for the form psychotic phenomena assume. The content results from the transformation of the pre-psychotic conflict as a result of the "reactions" (primary process) of the "undifferentiated state" (Katan, 1979). For example a patient who, prior to a psychotic attack (pre-psychotic phase), unconsciously envied his brother and wished to acquire all he possessed, had the delusion during the psychotic attack that his brother envied him and was trying to destroy him.

Arlow and Brenner, Pao, and Katan argue that unconscious conflict reaches an intensity that leads to a partial or complete dissolution of the ego organization. They differ in one fundamental respect. For Arlow and Brenner and for Pao, the formal aspects of the clinical phenomena (for example, transitivism, negativism) give expression to elements of interpersonal and endopsychic object relations. When a patient is engaged in a psychotherapeutic enterprise, transferences find expression through the medium of these disorders of form. This is not possible, according to Katan (1979), because object ties of any kind do not exist in the "undifferentiated state". The form of the clinical phenomena, cannot therefore, give representation to interpersonal and endopsychic object relations. Transferences cannot emerge, other than those that spring from the part of the mind unaffected by the morbid process (Katan, 1954).

The Kleinian concept of unconscious phantasy offers an alternative solution to the problem of the relationship between the form and content of psychotic phenomena. As endopsychic object relations, anxieties, and defences comprise the content of unconscious phantasies, their sensorimotor nature affords them their form. Sensations of biting, chewing, cutting, and mutilating the desirable and envied object and penetrating it, in a concrete fashion, are features specific to the paranoid–schizoid position. These "bad" aspects of the ego are countered by measures whose aim is to protect the "good" satisfying internalized part or whole object. This protection (defence) is provided by the same means (unconscious phantasies) as are employed in the sadistic attacks. Thus the ego is bitten and fragmented so that the "bad", dangerous elements within the self are separated (split) from the "good" parts. The drive to penetrate the object is used to expel these destructive parts of the self and locate them in objects (projective identification). Under the best circumstances these primitive endopsychic object relations become modified, contributing to healthy mental development. However, constitutional and environmental influences may result in a pathological development that predisposes to mental illness in later life. The form and the content of schizophrenic phenomena, for example, result from pathologically enhanced unconscious phantasies. Excessive splitting of the ego imparts this pathological quality. Apathy, loss of the sense of identity, and autonomy of the self are consequences of this fragmentation of the ego.

The concept of unconscious phantasy is also offered as an explanation for wish (grandiose) delusions. Apart from maniacal states, these delusions may appear at the onset of a schizophrenic psychosis or accompany or precede persecutory phenomena. They are to be found regularly in chronicity ("end states"—M. Bleuler, 1978). In terms of the Kleinian theory, they are a reaction to a psychical reality in which "good" objects have been attacked and destroyed. Omnipotence is the source of a reparation that restores the damaged objects. The wish delusions thus attenuate the virulence of the sadistic phantasies and relieve anxiety. That reparative phantasies play a part in the psychopathogenesis of the schizophrenias follows from the theory that the depressive position has had a tenuous development in these conditions (Segal, 1956).

A perspective on the theories

The theories presented to account for the form of psychotic phenomena do not sit easily together. Fundamental incompatibilities exist. Arlow and Brenner (1969), Pao (1979), and Katan (1979) propose that the change in form is attributable to psychical dissolution. Allowing for their differences about the fate of the ego organization, they agree that until the onset of the psychosis primitive defences (Arlow & Brenner, 1969) or reactions of the "undifferentiated state" (Katan, 1979) played no significant part in the patient's mental life. In the Kleinian theory the endopsychic object relations that constitute the pathological paranoid–schizoid position were ever-present elements from infancy onwards. These unconscious phantasies are not left behind.

In the psychoses delusional thinking replaces reality-orientated (voluntary) thought. Hallucinations replace percepts of all kinds. Arlow and Brenner (1969) claim that this is because the ego has lost the capacity to test reality. This explanation is not satisfactory. It leaves the unanswered question—how is reality testing lost? By using Freud's (1900a) theory of the dream as a model, it is possible to enter more deeply into this issue. As in sleep, the movement and distribution of instinctual cathexes (unconscious non-verbal mental events) (see Chapter 1) in the "undifferentiated state" is governed by the primary process (Katan's "reactions"). With external reality no longer available as a satisfying outlet for these cathexes, they can, as in the dream, only pursue a retrogressive course (topographic regression—Freud, 1900a). It is this movement that leads to the cathexis of phantasies and memories that act as substitutes (see Chapter 1), through displacement, for the anxiety-provoking object relations of the pre-psychotic phase (Katan, 1979). The ego system *Pcpt–Cs*, already disengaged from external reality, is turned to the now hypercathected contents. As belief in reality is inexplicably bound up with the senses, phantasy becomes delusion. Hallucinatory phenomena are explicable in the same manner. The retreating current of cathexis invests memory traces, which then regain their original perceptual quality. This contrasts with the waking state of the mentally healthy, where memories are never replaced by their perceptual source.

The loss of reality testing, according to the Kleinian theory, follows from the vicissitudes of unconscious phantasy. The unconscious phantasies that give the clinical phenomena their specific form have a defensive aim—to spare what remains of the ego and "good" objects from disintegration. Concomitantly, the defensive splitting and projective identification weaken the ego, leaving it in greater danger of fragmentation. Steiner's (1993) concept of "psychotic organizations of the personality" describes the psychical complexes constructed to relieve anxieties springing from the threat to the ego. Omnipotent reparative phantasies restore the damage done to the ego and to the objects. The delusional world so created is idealized and strenuously defended against rational considerations, despite its often persecutory nature.

According to the Kleinian theory, hallucinations occur when cognition (thinking, perceiving, attending, etc.) is drawn into the defensive struggle against unconscious phantasies springing from the death instinct. To spare the ego from experiencing the hated and feared internal and external reality, the cognitive ego is split up, fragmented, and projected into objects (Bion, 1959). The split-off "particles" of cognition may engulf the objects themselves. The schizophrenic patient's speech, thoughts, and memories are then experienced as existing and emanating from an external object (hallucinations).

Theories and the empirical data

For theories to have credibility, their concepts must be close to the empirical data. Clinical theories appear to meet this demand. They can dispense with concepts that seem to be distant from the phenomena encountered in clinical practice. Thus theories that account for psychotic phenomena on the basis of the defence concept (Arlow & Brenner, 1969; Pao, 1979; Steiner, 1993) have their foundations in the intrapsychic and interpersonal conflicts that abound in the utterances of psychotic patients. Nevertheless, there are attendant dangers when using the concepts of clinical theories alone. First and most immediate is the danger of overextending the use of the dynamic concept (conflict) as explanatory for the entire symptomatology and courses of psychotic illness.

This danger of overextension is most apparent in the theories of Arlow and Brenner (1969), Bion (1959), Pao (1979), Klein (1946), and Rosenfeld (1954). Concentrating on single cases militates against recognition of the wide variations that exist within and between clinical types, with regard both to symptoms and to courses of illness (London, 1973). In the theories referred to, little distinction, as to symptom formation, is made between the phenomena that occur in recent and long-standing cases. When schizophrenias proceed to chronicity, the delusional content is different from that which was present at the onset (Bleuler, 1911). The exception is the periodic acute persecutory attacks, which today are mostly alleviated by chemotherapy.

The wish delusions of chronicity, based on adolescent erotic and ambitious phantasies, offer comfort to the patient by reversing a disagreeable, frustrating reality and a sense of helplessness (see Chapter 1). However, psychoanalysts are then inclined to regard all delusions as the product of a defence, either against instinctual derivatives or to prevent fragmentation of the ego. Yet in the chronic schizophrenias, particularly in the hebephrenic–catatonic type, delusions do not shore up a disintegrating ego, because already there is fragmentation of cognition and impoverishment of the self. The argument in favour of a defensive process is more easily sustained in those cases of recent onset where the delusional content reveals the presence of conflict. Once delusions are formed and established, they appear to "fill in" the gaps left by the loss of realistically based relationships with others—Freud's (1911c) concept of restitution. It is as if a process of recovery (repair) has gone awry.

There is another cause for discontent with clinical theories. They tend to neglect the economic factor in mental life (see Chapter 1). It is well known, for example, that psychopharmacological treatments, hormone therapy, ageing, and other unknown mental changes lead to conscious phantasies losing their affective qualities and drive to action, while their ideational content retains its place in consciousness. Here it is a matter of mental economics, not dynamics. Katan' s (1979) metapsychological theory, which limits the defensive (dynamic) struggle to the pre-psychotic phase alone (Katan, 1954), corrects this lack by emphasizing the importance of mental economics in the creation of delusions and hallucinations.

If a theory has substance it should contribute to the technique of treatment. This, as has been seen (Chapter 5), is particularly apposite in Kleinian theory. By contrast the Katan approach, following Federn (1953) and others, is limited to encouraging the restoration of object ties with the aim of enabling the patient to correct his falsifications of thought, perception, and memory.

Theories designed to account for the form of psychotic phenomena cannot appeal to good therapeutic results to support claims of validity. Interpretative and other types of intervention based on a variety of theories of psychopathogenesis may lead to a remission of symptoms. Just as often, these interventions fail to affect the process of illness. This is the usual outcome in established cases of schizophrenia. Additionally, there is the fact that spontaneous remission was commonplace before the advent of physical treatments. These observations cast doubt on the claim, in the psychoses, that therapeutic benefit can only follow the application of a technique based on a particular psychological theory of causation.

Sufficient has been written to show that the explanatory concepts belonging to different theories are incompatible with one another, despite their relative allegiance to the role of conflict. Each theory offers a comprehensive explanation of the manner of formation of the clinical phenomena. None assists in improving forecasts for the course of illness (prognosis), nor provides a uniformly effective method of psychological treatment.

CHAPTER TEN

Theory and technique in psychoanalysis

Today, psychoanalysis is not practised in accordance with a uniform set of technical procedures. Each psychoanalyst encourages his patient to follow the rule of free association. This varies in the importance and significance attached to these associations. The different techniques are closely related to theories of psychopathogenesis and the psychoanalytic process.

The technique of resistance (defence) analysis

In its beginnings, psychoanalytic practice was an entirely empirical procedure. Following Breuer's exceptional experience with Anna O. (Breuer, 1895a), he found, with Freud and with Janet (1893), that hypnotized patients who suffered from hysteria (paralyses, absences, clouding of consciousness, amnesia) spontaneously recalled experiences of a traumatic kind that had preceded the onset of the illness. If the recall comprised the affect as well as the ideation belonging to the traumatic event, symptomatic relief followed. Following these observations, Freud and Breuer (1895d) described a theory to account for the formation of hysterical symptoms. These symptoms occurred in predisposed individuals when memories of traumatic events were purposively or automatically dismissed from consciousness, along with the associated affect. The release of affect that accompanied the recall (abreaction) was responsible for the disappearance of the symptoms.

The technique of treatment now followed the theory. It took the form of an active search for memories of traumatic events. Memories of this kind were not easily disclosed, and so Freud (1898a) concluded that patients harboured a resistance against remembering emotionally painful experiences. He also discovered that a source of resistance against the successful pursuance of the treatment was the presence of "false connections", that is, transferences. When patients failed to respond symptomatically to the recovery of memories of recent traumatic events, Freud (1898a) extended this search to puberty and pre-puberty. Gradually he altered his technique. He abandoned hypnosis and the procedure of exhorting his patients to remember and substituted the method of free association. In the course of his search for traumatic events in childhood, he came to report (1898a) that many of his female patients had been seduced by their fathers. However, as Schimek (1975) has shown, the majority of these patients did not have conscious memories of being seduced. Rather, they reported memories and thoughts that Freud (1896b) described as follows: "their traces are never present in conscious memories, only in the symptoms of the illness". In making these reconstructions, Freud (1896c) followed the procedure he used in the interpretation of dreams.

The method of free association led to a plethora of new data and to recognition of the extent to which phantasies comprised the patients' thought material. This led Freud (1916–17) to describe a more detailed theory of hysterical and obsessional neuroses. These neuroses were precipitated by the frustration of sexual wish phantasies or by fear of them. Failing to find an outlet, the libido regresses to previous forms of satisfaction—". . . under the double threat of external and internal frustration it (libido) becomes refractory and recalls earlier and better times" (Freud, 1916–17). These "earlier and better" times are the satisfactions gained from the love objects of childhood and the component instincts (scoptophilia, exhibitionism, etc.). The data on which the hypothesis of a return to "earlier and better times" rests were described in Chapter 2 (see the case of Mr A). The resistance that patients exert against the recollection of these childhood sexual wishes and phantasies reflects the extent to which they are no longer acceptable to adult standards. The patient who succumbs to an hysterical neurosis resolves the unconscious conflict between the regressed wishes and the adult personality by creating symptoms that satisfy both the unacceptable childhood wishes and the opposition to them. Symptoms are a compromise formation.

Experience with the symptom neuroses (hysterias, obsessional neuroses) revealed to Freud that the transference was one of the most important causes of resistance. In the typical case, the psychoanalyst became the focus of the patient's childhood object relations. The waning of symptoms was accompanied by the patient living through the gamut of emotions belonging with these object relations. The real neurosis, Freud (1916–17) believed, had been replaced by a transference neurosis. The resolution of the symptoms, i.e. the resolution of the conflict, could now be undertaken within the analytic situation.

In Freud's (1919a) words, the therapeutic task consists ". . . of two things: making conscious the repressed instinctual material and uncovering the resistances". From a theoretical standpoint, based on typical cases, therapeutic benefit depended on the dissolution of these resistances, of which the patient was unaware. The prerequisite for this dissolution was a strong attachment to the psychoanalyst and a reasonable residue of healthy mental life. For the psychoanalyst's sake, the patient was prepared to undergo the discomforts that the resistances caused. The help the psychoanalyst could give was to interpret the resistance.

The theory of symptom formation in the neuroses required the dissolution of resistances if the patient's recovery was to be effected. Thus, when faced with the fact that all cases are not ideal cases, Freud (1919a) decided that some patients needed the analysts help to conquer the resistances. This required more activity on the analyst's part than mere interpretation if the patient were to reach that state of mind when there could be a resolution of conflict. Freud (1919a) wrote: "I think activity on the part of the analysing physician is unobjectionable and entirely justified." At this time (1919), cases of symptom neurosis no longer constituted the majority of patients in analysis. Although many patients presented with neurotic symptoms, it soon became apparent that they were the expression of a character abnormality. In these cases the reclamation of repressed wishes was not effective therapeutically. For this reason, perhaps, Freud reminded analysts that his analytic technique had followed from the neuroses. It must be, he states, that ". . . another quite different kind of activity is necessitated by the gradually growing appreciation that the various forms of disease treated by us cannot all be dealt with by the same technique" (Freud, 1919a) .

The introduction of the "structural theory" may be seen in the light of therapeutic encounters with patients suffering from character abnormalities and depressive states. In both, a negative therapeutic reaction was often the rule (see Chapter 3). This reaction persisted despite the analysis of resistances, of a negative attitude to the analyst, and of recognition of the role of secondary gain (Freud, 1923b). Freud hypothesized that the patient was unable to give up the illness because it satisfied a sense of guilt. The patient was unaware of this guilt: "he [the patient] did not feel guilty, he feels ill" (Freud, 1923b). It was likely that this unconscious sense of guilt was also present in neuroses. This conclusion on Freud's part led him to the theory of the (unconscious) superego. The theory was to have an important influence on technique. To resolve unconscious resistances against repressed wishes was now only part of the therapeutic work. Equally important was the task of uncovering the unconscious guilt and its causes.

The "structural" theory also facilitated a new theoretical perspective on the psychoanalysis of character and its abnormalities. The reintroduction of the concept of defence (Freud, 1926d) now became a means of discerning the sources and features of character traits. A variety of defences was at the disposal of the ego organization and could be deployed against dangers caused by the mental derivatives of instinct, by object loss, by the threat of object loss, and by the superego. In this context a character trait encapsulated a specific ego defence and a specific instinctual derivative. Thus repression, reaction formation, projection, etc. gave the trait its particular characteristics. The defence in question became an integral element of the personality—sometimes syntonic, at other times dystonic. Like the symptoms of a neurosis, a character trait could be regarded as a compromise formation (Yorke et al., 1989). However, there was an important difference. The compromise achieved by the neurotic conflict followed an unexpected danger arising in adolescence or adult life. In the case of a character trait, the danger having arisen in early life had been neutralized—hence the absence of the anxiety, which the neurotic compromise is unable to dispel except in hysterical conversion.

The consequences of these theoretical considerations are portrayed in Anna Freud's (1936) book, *The Ego and the Mechanisms of Defence*. Her concept of the transference of defence may be taken as illustrative. This defence, in the form of a character trait, is played out in the analysis. She describes her approach as follows: "I think that in such a case the analyst ought not to omit all the intermediate stages in the transformation which the instinct has undergone and endeavour at all costs to arrive directly at the primitive instinctual impulse against which the ego has set up its defence and to introduce it directly into consciousness. The more correct method is to change the focus of attention in the analysis, shifting it in the first place from the instinct to the specific method of defence i.e. from the id to the ego" (A. Freud, 1936). With an established theoretical base, resistance analysis was applicable to character abnormalities as well as to symptom neuroses (Fenichel, 1941; Glover, 1955).

By its very nature, resistance or defence analysis is a technique that takes as its ideal the empirical tradition in psychoanalysis that began with Freud's (1896b) explorations into hysterical neuroses. According to the technique, preconceived ideas about the meaning of the patient's utterances are to be eschewed until there is confirmation that the analyst is on the right track. Here memories, phantasies, and dreams play a role as important as the transference (Couch, 1995). The aim of the treatment is to allow the patient to produce this material on his own account through the analysis of resistances springing from the transference, ego, superego, and the id (Fenichel, 1941). It is perhaps pertinent to be reminded of Ferenczi and Rank's (1925) warning: "The analyst should not impart the theoretic knowledge which 'occurs' to him in connection with the association material of the patient; that is he should not express, as it were, his own parallel associations, but he should work over the whole material in himself and only impart that which the patient absolutely requires for the analytic experience, and its understanding."

Sandler (1992) took the opportunity to emphasize the importance of respecting the resistances that patients present during analytic treatment. Too often neglected is the self-preservative element inherent in a resistance, whatever its form: "The self-preservative aspect of resistance can be thought of as a form of intrapsychic adaptation to unpleasant affects including that which we know best as anxiety, shame, and guilt" (Sandler, 1992). Recognition of the self-preservative aspect of resistance, whatever its source, will dictate the manner in which the resistance is dealt with. Neglect of the self-preservative aspect by too direct an interpretation of the resistance brings with it the danger of the analyst being turned into ". . . a sort of moral censor who reproaches the patient for being bad" (Sandler, 1992).

Sandler's caveat bears on the subject of countertransference. The technique of resistance analysis makes full allowance for the impact countertransferences may have on the course of an analysis. Countertransferences are defined as the analyst's unconscious responses to the patient (Glover, 1955; Reich, 1951), in contrast to the extended use of the term (see Heimann, 1960). Derivatives of these countertransferences may become conscious. Glover (1955) described these conscious responses as counterresistances, to distinguish them from unconscious transferences.

The Kleinian technique and its development

In Chapter 7 a detailed account was given of Abraham's (1924) theory of the growth of object love. The purpose of this was to illustrate the extent of Abraham's influence on Melanie Klein, who was his analysand. It is an influence that is clearly detectable in the content of her first (1932) psychopathological and developmental theories. These theories are referred to here because of their relevance for Klein's technique of treatment—a technique radically different from resistance analysis.

By following Abraham's (1924) theory that the love object is incorporated (introjected) orally, destroyed, and expelled (projected) via the anus (object=faeces) during the earliest stages of the growth of object love, Klein (1932) was able to put forward an explanation for the destructive attacks the children she was treating made upon their toys. The toys represented the parents and aspects of themselves. The parental objects, she hypothesized, had as prototypes the mother's breast and the father's penis. Klein (1932) discerned phantasies whose content consisted of attacks on the parents in coitus, attacks on the contents of the mother's body—babies and the father's penis—believed to have been incorporated by the mother orally during coitus. Reparative phantasies included all those actions that were directed towards restoring the damaged or killed objects.

Klein (1932) concluded that in the case of her child patients, the sadistic attacks were caused by oral greed and envy of the parents. The attacks on the self had their source in the attacked objects, now invested with the child's oral and anal sadism, which, having been introjected, formed a primitive superego. Fear of these "bad" part (breast, penis) and whole objects (parents) led to their being projected, with resultant dread of attack from without. It was not only the children's play, Klein (1932) believed, that led to the discovery of these phantasies. Equally important was the manner in which the children related to her (1932). This latter provided content for interpretations that eased the children's anxieties. The "persecutory" fears suggested to Klein that they were little different from the persecutory delusions of adult patients. These "anxiety situations" (the psychotic anxieties) were not, in Klein's (1932) opinion, simply a reaction to real oral frustration, object loss, or excessive stimulation. The sadistic phantasies and the "anxiety situations" were an innate element of the children's psychical constitution, enhanced by adverse environmental events. Disturbed children differed from mentally healthy children with respect to the intensity of the unconscious phantasies of the kind that she identified.

Klein's (1932) interpretation of the neurotically disturbed children's behaviour, based on Abraham's (1924) theory of the role of destructive (oral/anal–sadistic) hate, came to form the foundation of her analytic technique with adult patients. This was to be supplemented by a new explanatory concept whose antecedents may be found in Abraham's (1924) concept of anal expulsion of the part and whole objects. This additional concept is projective identification (see Chapters 7, 8, and 9). This followed Klein's (1946) theory that splitting affects the ego as well as objects (see Chapter 6). As described earlier, clinical phenomena could now be explained as resulting from the penetration of the object by fragments of the splintered ego. The importance of this new concept cannot be over-estimated. It was to become a fundamental element of Kleinian technique.

Kleinian technique is predicated on the theory that all relationships with others evoke and provide material for unconscious phantasies. Once the patient has entered into a commitment to undertake treatment, the analyst becomes inextricably involved with the unconscious phantasies. These unconscious phantasies determine the nature and quality of the transference. The hypothesis that the transference arises immediately on the basis of unconscious phantasy is different from the concept of transference described by Freud (1940a).

In Klein's (1957) theory, patients who participate in psychoanalytic treatment have a need to keep the analyst as a "good" object. This is an onerous and difficult intrapsychic task for the patient because the analyst is already the object of unconscious acquisitive and destructive phantasies. Envy of his possessions, powers, and status are the mainspring of these unconscious phantasies. Schizoid mechanisms are brought into play to preserve the analyst (see Chapter 8). Others outside the analysis become the focus of the transference hate, thus turning them into "bad" objects. They are also feared because they have been penetrated by parts of the ego that are destructive in themselves (projective identification). The wish to preserve the analyst as a protective and supportive figure is not successful because these repudiated, destructive parts of the ego are projected into him. He remains an object of fear. Simultaneously, attempts to repair the damage psychically inflicted on the analyst proceed via the manic defence (see Chapter 7). This reparation goes hand-in-hand with idealization.

In the Kleinian technique, the analyst must avoid those actions and interventions that might reinforce the patient's defences of splitting, projective identification, and omnipotence (manic defence). Reassurance of any kind must be avoided, so that the patient is given every opportunity to become aware of his unconscious transference phantasies of envy, greed, hate, and acquisitiveness. As long as the schizoid mechanisms and omnipotence are successful in keeping these unconscious phantasies at bay, the mechanisms will provide a constant source of resistance. Unconscious envy, for example, may lead to a devaluation of the analyst and to a denigration or failure to understand the content of his interpretations. The analyst's most important interventions are those that are concerned with the patient's unconscious transference phantasies. Transference interpretations help the patient to abandon his need to split his objects into "good" and "bad". Equally, they allow him to reintegrate aspects of himself that he has projected into others.

The work of Rosenfeld (1952, 1954, 1987) and Bion (1959, 1962) with schizophrenic patients led to the theory of schizoid mechanisms achieving greater prominence in the technique of treatment. Bion's (1959, 1962) clinical experience led to his formulating a theory of infantile mental development that owed much to the way he interpreted the behaviour of his patients (see below). Faced with unresponsiveness, inappropriate utterances, and reactions to his interpretations, Bion (1959) turned to an explanation based on splitting and projective identification (schizoid mechanisms). He decided that the cause of the patient's behaviour resulted from a compulsive need to invest him (Bion) with specific mental contents (projective identification). This need blocked their ability to acknowledge and respond to his interventions. By insisting on presenting his interpretations, Bion believed that he effectively rejected what they wished him to experience. The repeated attempts on the patients' part to resort to projective identification suggested that they had been deprived of the benefits that this mechanism may afford. A resolution of the patient's difficulties might be achieved if the patient were helped to put his noxious "projections" into the analyst. In doing so, the projected material was attenuated and thus suitable for re-introjection. When this occurred a link could be established with the analyst. Destruction of links on all levels of mental functioning—sensorimotor, perceptual, conceptual—were damaged in the schizophrenias (Bion, 1959).

Healthy mental development, Bion (1959, 1962) proposed, depended on the creation of a link between the infant and his mother. This was contingent on the free play of projective identification. Under the best circumstances, the mother comes to serve as a repository for those psychical experiences the infant cannot manage for himself. Once the mother receives them into herself, they are "detoxified" and rendered into a state where the infant can introject them. Projective identification thus results in a satisfying emotional interchange between mother and infant. When the link is threatened by the infant's envy of the breast, there is a danger of that interchange being irrevocably damaged. If the mother cannot accept the infant's projections, a similar threat to the link is created. In seeing projective identification in this way, Bion (1959) and Rosenfeld (1987) removed its pathological association. "Good" as well as "bad" mental content are projected into others. Seeing oneself in the other facilitates understanding and sympathy. Empathy is thus understood as a result of "good" projective identification. In Bion's theory, the analyst as a container for projections has had a major impact on the technique of many analysts in the United Kingdom.

The technical innovations based on the theory of schizoid mechanisms were accompanied by a renewal of interest in the countertransference. Heimann (1960) was among the first to extend the meaning of the concept. It was her opinion that the countertransference was inadequately described if it were confined to the analyst's unconscious reactions to the patient. The concept should encompass the analyst's conscious as well as unconscious reactions (Heimann, 1960). Her original idea was that countertransference should not be thought of as disadvantageous to the analysis. Rather that ". . . the analyst's emotional response to the patient within the analytic situation represents one of the important tools for his work" (Heimann, 1950). This is possible because the analyst's conscious reactions to the patient are a response to the patient's unconscious preoccupations at that moment in time. Most significantly, Heimann (1960) asserted that the analyst's countertransference is not part of the analytic relationship but is the patient's creation. Heimann (1960) understood countertransference in its widest meaning as an expression of the patient's projective identifications. The countertransference, Heimann (1960) believed, was of the greatest value when the progress of an analysis was impeded or blocked. On such occasions the analyst, through his countertransference, could make contact with the helplessness, frustration, apathy, and anger that the patient was unable to feel. The patient was forcing the analyst, through his projections, to experience and live through these affects: "Now you know what its like," the patient seemed to be saying. It was essential, Heimann (1960) wrote, that the analyst must always examine his reactions to the patient closely before using them as material for interpretation. It was important to exclude influences drawn from some aspect of his personality, or from some real reaction to the patient.

The use of the countertransference as a means of "deepening" an analysis through interpretation based on it has become a central feature of Kleinian technique. Attention is focused on the unconscious interchanges occurring between patient and analyst. The patient is constantly exerting pressure (projective identification) on the analyst to enact roles from his internal world. This requires a refinement of technique. It has been described by Feldman (1997) as follows: "more recently, a number of authors have been concerned to elaborate the concept of countertransference with what is described as an intersubjective model of psychoanalysis, where the emphasis is on the significance of the analyst's own subjective experiences in his understanding of and his method of responding to the patient".

Fairbairn and the object relations school

It is hardly an exaggeration to claim that Fairbairn's contributions (1940, 1944) to theory and technique have provided the foundation for the object relations school of the British Psychoanalytical Society (Kohon, 1986)—notwithstanding the pioneering work of Ferenczi (1928) or the later contributions of Balint (1968) and Winnicott (1965). Fairbairn (1940) was impressed by the manner in which patients related to him and the significance they attributed to the relationship. This overshadowed whatever other mental contents the patient made available in the analysis, either directly or as a result of his interventions. Fairbairn (1940) observed that his patients were fearful of the demands they made on him. They feared his disapproval. They reacted to weekends and other breaks in the analysis with fear and anger. Fairbairn (1940) was struck by their concern that they had exhausted him because they were unsatisfied by his efforts to help them. They felt endangered by an insatiable hunger and destructive greed. By isolating themselves from others—and from Fairbairn also—they could ensure the safety of their love objects. Thus they had to turn to phantasy for consolation. Omnipotent phantasies either overt or latent were characteristic. Fairbairn (1940) concluded that his patient's relationships with him were principally determined by wishes for and fear of dependence on the one hand, and wishes for and fear of independence on the other.

Fairbairn (1940) attributed to a split in the ego patients' ability to tolerate contradictory attitudes to reality, to the self, and to others (see Chapters 6 and 7). This splitting (schizoid position) was least obvious in the symptom neuroses. It was most apparent in hysterical amnesic states, in hysterical personality types, and in the schizophrenias. Splitting was the means whereby the patient could deal with the anxiety provoked by transference thoughts and affects. Through splitting, the "good" and "bad" parts of the self could be separated. If "good", the patient would be tolerated by Fairbairn. Equally, Fairbairn was split, so that he could be perceived as "good" while his frightening "bad" objects (frustrating, exciting) were displaced to others. The patient's transferences provided the material for Fairbairn's (1944) theory that the transferences were an expression of endopsychic object relations in which "exciting" and "rejecting" objects and ego structures (central ego, libidinal ego, anti-libidinal ego) interacted with one another. The predisposition and immediate cause of mental disorders were to be found in disturbances affecting endopsychic object relations—not, as Freud (1916–17) proposed, from an unconscious conflict between unacceptable (childhood) wishes and the adult personality.

Fairbairn's theory led to a radical revision of his psychoanalytic technique. Clinical experiences led him to conclude that from a therapeutic viewpoint, interpretation was not, of itself, a sufficient instrument for psychical change (Fairbairn, 1958). He reasoned that as the patient's difficulties arose from an unsatisfying and disappointing childhood relationship with the mother heightened in inner (psychical) reality, the relationship with the analyst must assume decisive importance therapeutically. The analyst as a real person is in a position to bring about a beneficial alteration to the patient's endopsychic state. What had been denied to the patient in his early childhood could be rectified in his relationship with the analyst. An opportunity was afforded for psychical maturation. If such an aim were to be successfully pursued, changes had to be made to the psychoanalytic method. Fairbairn (1958) believed that the method as practised contained anti-therapeutic elements. The requirements that the patient should assume a recumbent position on the couch and the demand for free associations only encouraged the revival of childhood traumatic events, thus heightening resistances.

The primary aim of psychoanalytic technique, according to Fairbairn's theory (1944), is to bring about a synthesis of the personality by reducing the degree of splitting. This is difficult because of the patient's unconscious resistance to an alteration in the psychical "status quo". There is an unconscious need on the patient's part to retain his aggression in an internalized state, so that the external object is protected. This requires that the early splitting of the internalized object (mother) into a "good" and "bad" object is maintained (see Chapter 6). An intrapsychic "closed system" has evolved, which perpetuates the relationship between the various ego attitudes and their respective internal objects, as well as between one another. The principal purpose of treatment is to effect breaches of the "closed system" and make the inner world accessible to outer reality (Fairbairn, 1958).

It was Fairbairn's opinion (1958) that transference interpretations were so often disappointing therapeutically because the phenomena of the transference were expressions of the "closed system". For therapeutic change to occur, a relationship between analyst and patient in the real world must be established. This results in a break in the "closed system" within which the patient's symptoms have developed and been maintained. The establishment of an "open system" allows the possibility of a correction of the abnormal endopsychic object relations and permits realistic relations with external objects. It follows from this that the analyst must abandon the detachment insisted upon by the traditional

analytic method and appear as a real person. The analyst's interventions must be designed to overcome the patient's unconscious
efforts to force the analyst into the "closed system" through encouraging transferences. Transferences act to oppose the analytic
process, unless they are identified for what they are—expressions
of the "closed system". Fairbairn advocated that those requirements that are part of the conventional psychoanalytic method
must be modified or abandoned. To enable the patient to see the
analyst as a real person, Fairbairn stopped asking his patients to lie
on the couch, nor did he sit behind them. Instead, he had the
patient sit upright with the chair parallel to his. These measures
were to facilitate the process whereby the patient could come to
accept "the open system of reality" (Fairbairn, 1958).

Those who align themselves with Fairbairn's (1944) theory of
endopsychic object relations have not used his nomenclature to
describe internal objects and ego structures. They have, however,
made free use of his concept of splitting and Klein's (1940, 1946)
concepts of schizoid mechanisms and the depressive position.
There is support for Fairbairn's (1944) assertion that the development of sexuality, in all its expressions, ultimately depends upon
an optimal evolution of endopsychic object relations.

In general, the object relations school identifies with Fairbairn
in rejecting the body as a primary source of pleasure. The erotogenic zones reach significance when object relations are frustrating
and disappointing. The role of sexuality in promoting conflict is
diminished. Whether erotogeneity is primary or secondary may be
explored by taking the instance of the character trait of negativism.
This trait may become manifest during psychoanalytic treatment,
causing considerable resistance. According to Freud's (1905d)
theory of sexuality, this trait has its source in a fixation at the anal
erotogenic zone. This hypothesis is based on psychoanalytic facts
that indicate that the child obtained pleasure from holding back
his stool. This is heightened by the inability of the mother, through
lack of knowledge or insensitivity, to help the child to renounce
the pleasure. The reaction to the mother's demand to release the
stool was "No". This is repeated as a transference. Object relations
analysts find the cause for the anal retentiveness and the later
negativism, not in the wish for bodily (anal) pleasure, but in a
disturbed relationship with the mother. If there had been a harmo-

nious relationship with the mother, there would have been no reason to hold on to the stool. The disturbed relationship is internalized only to find expression again in analysis.

The theory that the cause of unconscious conflict lies in disturbed endopsychic object relations is the basis of the treatment technique. To reach these conflicts and resolve the disordered object relations, the analyst's task must be to discover the ways in which the patient is reacting to him. These reactions are subtly expressed but, when found, provide the "material" for transference interpretations. There is the assumption that by following the "here-and-now" approach, affects will not be overlooked, as may be the case when emphasis is laid on the retrieval of memories. It is claimed that memories that are significant for the neurotic state will make a spontaneous appearance following the work in the transference. Kohon (1986) has described the object relations perspective on the analytic process as follows: "the psychoanalytic situation is always created and developed from the specific and unique interaction between the patient and the analyst. The analyst is never an outsider; he is part and parcel of the transference situation." This interpretation of the analytic process owes much to the object relations orientation of Kleinian theory. It is in their emphasis on the transference–countertransference interaction that the object relations analysts part company with Fairbairn (1958). He could not free himself from the suspicion that the transference embodies anti-therapeutic influences (suggestibility and dependency).

It would give an erroneous impression of the object relations technique if it were thought to be a method exclusively devoted to work in the transference. Klauber (1976), following Fairbairn closer than he may have realized, deprecated an impassive and unresponsive attitude on the part of the analyst. This, as Kohut was to claim, may be a cause of resistance. A "Jehovah-like stance" (Klauber, 1976) only results in blocking the patient's capacity for affect expression.

Attention to the countertransference is an indispensable part of the object relations technique. Here again some object relations analysts are cautious in using it as a therapeutic tool, because of doubts about its possible sources (Bollas, 1979). All conscious countertransference reactions need not be the result of projective identification. The object relations school's theory is that the analytic process may offer the patient an opportunity to restore his ego, which has been weakened by splits and fragmentation. The outcome of treatment will depend on the extent of this damage, which has resulted from adverse childhood environmental events and their psychical repercussions. This theory of psychopathogenesis has been conceptualized in terms of Fairbairn's (1940) "schizoid position", Balint's (1968) "basic fault", and Winnicott's (1965) "true and false self".

Kohut's technique of treatment

Kohut's (1971, 1977) technique of treatment is based on theoretical assumptions. A brief account of his work with "narcissistic" patients that led to his developmental theory was given in Chapter 8. Kohut (1971, 1977) found that the progress of his patients was not enhanced through the analysis of transference or of ego or superego resistances. The exposure of conflict did not lead to therapeutic improvement. These observations led Kohut (1971, 1977) to query the importance of uncovering resistances and to doubt the technique employed to achieve this (resistance analysis). It appeared to him that the analytic data that are interpreted as resulting from fixations to pregenital sexual organizations and to incestuous objects or data explained as the expression of aggression are the consequence of a self that has failed to develop. It is an "enfeebled" self (Kohut, 1971) that has never had a healthy self-assertiveness in relation to a mirroring self-object and an admiration for an idealized self-object (see chapter 8). The result is a defensive turning-away to pleasure through the medium of the erotogenic zones or to aggression. Kohut and Fairbairn relegate the role of instinctual derivatives to a secondary position.

Kohut's theory that failure of the self to develop satisfactorily results from "empathy failure" (Kohut, 1977) on the part of the parental self-objects has important implications for analytic technique, especially for the way in which the interpretation of content and resistance should be made. According to Kohut (1971), there must be two phases in each interpretation. The first consists of ensuring that the patient feels that the therapist fully appreciates and understands what has been said to him. Once this has been achieved, it is appropriate to communicate the essential content of the interpretation. Failure to manage the first phase successfully is the cause of the most intractable resistances. In such an instance the analyst has behaved similarly to the parent who did not meet the patient's need in childhood for an "empathic echo or merger" with the self-object (Kohut, 1977). The patient requires a long period of being understood before the second phase of an interpretation is entered upon. The major resistances encountered during analytic treatment are, therefore, not due to the fear of repressed wishes, the strictures of the superego, or separation anxiety. Resistances are inadvertently caused by the analyst rigidly adhering to the conflict theory of neuroses. The analyst makes interventions that are experienced as traumatic by the patient—as traumatic as the parents' inability to understand, appreciate, and respond to the emotional needs of the patient in his childhood.

The Kohutian analysis offers the patient opportunity for the self to grow and develop. The self-object, which the analyst becomes, is not separate from the patient's self, but is an intrinsic part of it. The transferences that appear (idealizing, mirror) are not used for the purposes of imparting knowledge to the patient. The analyst does not address himself to an ego he believes to be intact. Instead, these transferences become the material for the "transmuting internalizations" that will modify the infantile libidinal constellations (idealized parental imago and the grandiose self). This allows the self to become resilient and stable and to permit a realistic perception of others. The analysis, when successful, has repaired the damage inflicted on the developing self in childhood by unempathic parents.

On the viability of the analytic process

On what does the viability of a psychoanalytic treatment depend? What keeps the treatment in progress when the patient has to face anxieties and guilt "reactions"? The patient's ability to persist and co-operate is clearly independent of the specific technique the analyst employs (Wallerstein, 1990). It makes little difference whether the analyst favours resistance analysis, object relations analysis, or the techniques of Klein and Kohut. There must be a factor common to the different methods. Some insight into this common factor may be gained from an examination of those patients whose mental illness prevents their participating in analytic treatment. Two clinical categories will be considered here: (1) cases of schizophrenia that have reached an "end state" (Bleuler, 1978) and (2) those types of mental illness that manifest themselves in disturbances of bodily sensation—for example, the dysmorphophobias. Patients suffering from these illnesses have a delusion-like belief in the organic nature of their complaint—hence the fact that they are often categorized within the group of borderline states. They are to be distinguished, however, from those borderline states that are characterized by impulsive and self-destructive behaviour and by neurotic symptoms including depersonalization and derealization.

Why do dysmorphophobic patients refuse to consider that their illness has a psychical basis? When these patients agree to begin treatment, why do they bring it to an end after such a short time? Why are schizophrenic patients so difficult to treat psychotherapeutically (Lucas, 1985)? Is it due to the psychoanalysts' limited understanding of the psychopathology? Is it due to the psychical situation existing between analyst and patient? Has the analyst, as some would claim, failed to make those interpretative interventions that would have safeguarded the viability of the treatment? When interpretations appear to be soundly based on empirical data, why do they not lead to the patient's commitment to the treatment process?

Individuals afflicted by the schizophrenias and the dysmorphophobias differ from those who suffer from symptom and character neuroses in one significant respect: they do not volunteer memories of their recent or distant past, nor do they disclose details of their phantasies. They confine what they have to say to their delusional experiences or, in the case of the dysmorphophobias, to their distressing bodily sensations. It may be that their memories and phantasies are embedded within their repeated complaints. There is some evidence in favour of this hypothesis. Patients in schizophrenic "end states" differ with respect to their ability and willingness to talk about themselves. Some who fall into the persecutory type of the illness may speak freely, especially about their delusional ideas. They may give the impression that they are ready to engage in psychotherapy. In fact, their aim is to find an ally who will help them fulfil their delusional ambitions or protect them from their persecutors. When disappointed in this, they lose interest and turn away. Other patients of the hebephrenic–catatonic type are quite different. They are inattentive, withdrawn, disinterested, neglectful of self, and sometimes negativistic. This variation between types warns against making generalizations about the mental pathology of the schizophrenias.

The situation encountered with dysmorphophobic patients is similar in many ways. They, too, are self-preoccupied, but it is with their disagreeable bodily sensations: the nose looks and feels too big or is misshapen; the hair has an unusual texture, which attracts critical attention; the lips have a peculiar shape; etc. This preoccupation leads to an egocentrism not unlike that found in the schizophrenias. Patients are intolerant of the suggestion that they may benefit if the emotional basis of their symptom could be discovered. Dysmorphophobias can continue unchanged over many years, with an eventual remission. In a very few cases the symptom loses some of its intensity, and then patients are less resistant to the idea of psychotherapy. It is in these cases that the cause of the choice of symptom may be discovered (Freeman, 1988; Freeman & Kells, 1996).

In long-standing cases of schizophrenia ("end states"), where regular contact has been maintained over a period of time, it becomes apparent that these patients are by no means insensitive to (the psychiatrist/analyst) whom they meet on a daily basis. The analyst becomes the object of a range of emotions whose expression is sporadic and fleeting. Anger, anxiety, envy, jealousy, concern, and sadness appear spontaneously or as reactions to events in the relationship. This is apart from the transitivism, aberrant concept formation, and so on that interfere with intelligible verbal communication. How are the expressions of affect understood? They seem to be no different from the affects encountered in the treatment of the neuroses. Yet their expression usually evokes an exacerbation of delusions or a profound withdrawal, either of which may temporarily or permanently bring the clinical contact to an end.

Dysmorphophobic patients always insist that talking about their illness is a waste of time: "Talking can't cure a broken arm." A few will agree to meet regularly, but this commitment is rarely upheld. A reason given is that they are reluctant to leave home because others will perceive their disfigurement. The anxiety this generates can cause them to remain in bed for days on end, inaccessible to all. When they do speak, it is to blame doctors for making their symptoms worse. They often vow revenge. Like schizophrenic patients, they appear indifferent to whomsoever has arranged to see them. There is never any direct criticism, but the analyst is left in no doubt about the patient's contempt for his puny therapeutic powers. In this there is a commonality with the schizophrenic patient. If the therapeutic contact can be continued over a long period, various affects appear, but again only sporadically. A wish for an exclusive relationship, jealousy of other patients, envy, fear of death wishes, and fears lest the analyst's self-confidence will be damaged are often followed by an intensification of the symptom and interruption of the treatment. This does not always herald an end to the meetings, but it may do so as with schizophrenic patients.

What have the different psychopathological theories to say about these clinical facts? Since Freud's studies on paranoiac psychoses, the phenomena of the schizophrenias have been explained in accordance with the hypothesis that unconscious mental conflict is at the heart of the symptomatology. The theories are based on the model Freud outlined for the neuroses. Freud's libidinal decathexis–recathexis (restitutional) theory (Freud, 1911c) had the aim of providing an understanding of the positive and negative aspects of schizophrenic autism. The content of delusions pointed to the pressure of conflict. The indifference to others and the pathological egocentrism indicated a lack of the potential for transference.

Federn (1953) discovered that some schizophrenic patients could engage in psychotherapy. He attributed this to their having made a positive transference to him. Other reactions of the kind described occurred. Sometimes this led to termination of the treatment. The fact that patients reacted to him in a positive or negative manner led Federn (1953) to propose, contrary to Freud's (1911c) theory, that objects did not lose their cathexis. He concluded that the psychopathological fault leading to the symptomatology consisted of a loss of ego cathexis and therefore of the ego boundary. The question remained: Does the potential for positive transference arise from the residues of the healthy adult mental life, or is it connected with reactions to the morbid process?

The theory of a redistribution of libidinal cathexis (Freud, 1911c) may also be applied to the dysmorphophobias and allied states (severe erythrophobia, hypochondriasis, etc.), although here the ego boundary remains intact. The egocentrism of the dysmorphophobias may be understood as the result of object cathexis being transported to the body. The object relations conflicts are dealt with by projection and externalization in the schizophrenias. In the dysmorphophobias the conflicts are dealt with by introjection of and identification with the love object. This theory emphasizes that the morbid process does not involve the whole of the patient's mental life. As in the schizophrenias, the strength of the remaining healthy mental life fluctuates throughout the course of the illness.

The theory of the schizophrenias given by Klein (1932, 1946) and developed by her co-workers (Bion, 1959; Rosenfeld, 1954) has already been described (see Chapters 7 and 8). The decathexis–recathexis theory was rejected on clinical grounds. Klein's defensive theory (Chapters 7 and 8) is similar to that proposed by Sullivan (1962) and followed by Fromm-Reichmann (1941), Knight (1953), and others. Klein's theory has had a major impact on many psychoanalysts working with schizophrenics and borderline patients. Her explanatory concepts have been incorporated into the theoretical formulations of Searles (1963), Grotstein (1977a, 1977b), Ogden (1980), and Kernberg (1984).

Those who interpret schizophrenic symptoms and behaviour as being the expression of pathological endopsychic object relations will explain the dysmorphophobias in a somewhat similar fashion. The pathological egocentrism is not the result of a narcissistic withdrawal—that is, a withdrawal of libido onto the bodily self. The vigorous rejection of psychotherapeutic help, the devaluation of the treatment, and the imagined damage caused by previous doctors may be attributed to unconscious phantasies (schizoid mechanisms) which now come to involve the analyst. Dysmorphophobic patients are encountered who fear that their lack of responsiveness will damage the analyst's self-confidence. Equally, here there are patients who believe that their symptom is due to bodily damage, self-inflicted by masturbation, or by some outside agency such as medical or dental treatment. These anxieties may explain why the patients react so badly to the suggestion of psychological treatment.

According to the endopsychic object relations theory, unconscious phantasies of having been injured by an internal object turned malignant by the patient's acquisitive greed are responsible for the dysmorphophobia. For example, a patient claimed that poison from a dental abscess, incorrectly treated, was the reason why one side of his face had changed in shape. The poison had sapped his energy and left him weak and impotent. It is possible to hypothesize that it was his envy and greed that had exhausted his objects. Now internalized, these objects, turned "bad", were attacking him from within with the poison (excreta) with which he had damaged the objects.

The extent to which clinical practice is guided by theory is seen in the case of the analytic approach to the treatment of severe mental illness. Those who approach the schizophrenic or dysmorphophobic patient in the hope that their presence, their sympathetic and understanding interest will strengthen what remains of healthy mental life do so because they adhere to the decathexis–recathexis theory. As the healthy mental processes strengthen, the patient may be able to recognize how he has falsified his thinking, perceiving, and remembering when under the influence of powerful affects. This work is done through the medium of the patient–analyst interaction. Persecutory delusions and hallucinations that attach themselves to the analyst are the main threat to the treatment. Experience has shown that frequency of sessions may be anti-therapeutic in that the interpersonal contact evokes too much anxiety. A judgement has to be made on the optimum number of sessions needed in each case.

What the analyst says to the patient is designed to help him feel that his fears about the treatment are understood. Initial interpretations have this aim. The analyst must be prepared for uncertainty. Patients are often silent, their utterances repetitive and difficult to understand. If signs of interest appear in the treatment, then opportunities may arise to make interpretations that connect a symptom or behaviour with an unacceptable idea or affect. The danger here is always that such attempts may lead to anxiety endangering the treatment process. When some progress in made, as judged by the patient's attitude, it is possible to identify the childhood object relations that have provided the basis for the emerging tie to the analyst that makes the treatment possible.

The therapeutic technique that follows the theory of unconscious (psychotic) transference phantasies is different. Delusional and affective reactions to the analyst in the case of the schizophrenias and manifestations characteristic of the dysmorphophobias are dealt with by making manifest, through interpretation, the unconscious transference phantasies that the personal contact has awakened. The patient's need to disengage from the hoped-for therapeutic relationship will gradually disappear as he recognizes that his morbid experiences (delusions, etc.) are a means of protecting self and good objects from destructive envy as expressed in unconscious phantasy. As interpretation is the therapeutic lever, there is no need to cultivate a positive attachment to the analyst or provide explanations or reassurance. On the contrary, the need is to bring the patient's hatred of reality—and therefore of the analyst—to the centre of the stage. A somewhat similar situation is hypothesized for the dysmorphophobias and borderline states.

This interpretative method has had its measure of success with cases of schizophrenia of recent onset, but, like the technique based on the decathexis theory, it has failed with patients whose illness has been of long standing. The failure to effect beneficial change has led those who believe in the centrality of a transference psychosis to revise aspects of their theoretical stance and thus to modify their therapeutic technique. This revision had its source in Bion's (1959) theory (see Chapter 8 and 9) that the schizophrenic patient hates reality so much that the cognitive processes that give it mental representation are attacked and destroyed. As described earlier, interpretations designed to give the patient insight into his disturbed psychical state and so ease his anxieties are ignored by him, misinterpreted, or angrily rejected. For example, Steiner (1993) describes a situation where he believed his interpretations to be correct, yet it was unhelpful—indeed "unbearable"—to the patient. In such circumstances the patient's wish that the analyst would understand his mental distress may be undermined by interpretative interventions. The same holds true for non-psychotic patients ". . . locked in the paranoid–schizoid position" (Joseph, 1983). To offset this harmful effect the analyst must help the patient to appreciate that his unbearable affective state is understood. Steiner (1993) calls this need "analyst-centred interpretations", in contrast to "patient-centred interpretations". His technique comes closer to that advocated by those who subscribe to the decathexis theory.

The challenge presented by the types of mental illness described here goes beyond the question of why only a small number of patients can be engaged in a full or modified psychoanalytic treatment. Clinical experience has shown that the schizophrenic or dysmorphophobic patient's responsiveness, or lack of it, is not dependent on a specific technique of treatment. It follows that the analyst's interventions, be they interpretative, explanatory, or reassuring, are not the decisive factor determining the patient's reactions to the treatment.

Clinical experience suggests that a positive reaction on the patient's part depends not on the specific content of the analyst's verbal interventions, but on the likelihood that he constitutes the principal therapeutic agent. For reasons not immediately obvious at the outset, the patient forms a bond with the analyst—a bond sufficiently strong to assimilate the strains of the affective reactions that inevitably arise in the course of treatment. Successfully treated cases (Freeman, 1988; Freeman & Kells, 1996) suggest that this bond is based on a secure and emotionally satisfying relationship in the patient's childhood. The analyst's interventions or his modifications of technique cannot bring this into being. Here clinical experiences part company with forecasts based on theory.

In patients suffering from symptom and character neuroses, a quite different situation exists. These patients are overwhelmingly responsive to their analysts, even if judged only by their commitment to the treatment, as evidenced by their consistent attendance. An effect of this responsiveness is to encourage analysts to believe that progress in the analysis and beneficial change in symptoms and behaviour come about solely as a result of interpretation—that despite the many contributions (Balint, 1968; Ferenczi, 1928; Winnicott, 1965) which emphasize the importance of non-interpretative influences for the outcome of psychoanalytic treatment. Predominant is the emotional tie to the analyst, not only as a transference object but as a real figure (Baker, 1993; Greenson, 1985).

In severe mental illness interpretations and their effects can be seen in a new light—one not so apparent in the case of the neuroses. By themselves, interpretations do not decide the fate of therapeutic efforts with schizophrenic or dysmorphophobic patients. This is determined by the patient's capacity to form a bond with the analyst. This clinical observation does not minimize or undervalue the crucial role that interpretation plays in freeing the neurotic patient from repressions or from gaining insight into disadvantageous character traits. Experiences with the severely mentally ill draw attention to the important influence of non-interpretative influences, particularly the presence of a tie to the analyst. This must be no less so in the case of the neuroses.

Each of the treatment methods described in this chapter follows distinct theoretical lines. Each technique is based on a theory of the psychopathogenesis of mental illness. To restore some order to these different views, Wallerstein (1990) argues that too much attention has been paid to the differences that exist between the content of interpretations favoured by each school. He suggests that the interpretations should be regarded as metaphors rather than as representing actual mental events that are dominating the patient's mind. What is common to all the techniques, Wallerstein (1990) believes, is the importance all analysts give to the movement of the transference and countertransference reactions.

Wallerstein's (1990) argument is consistent with the view that the viability of analytic treatment depends upon the patient's ability to form an attachment to the analyst. It is this attachment (positive transference) that enables the patient to reflect upon the analyst's interventions and not reject them out of hand. The analyst's consistency, maintained over a lengthy period of time, provides the basis for the growth of an attachment to him. The analytical process cannot advance unless the patient is able to reflect on his own thoughts and affects as well as experience them (Sterba, 1934). This ability allows the patient to join in the work. It is the basis for an identification with the analyst. There is a therapeutic alliance (Greenson, 1985). It is the identification with the analyst that enables the patient to continue a self-analysis after the treatment has ended. In character abnormalities and borderline states, the capacity to observe the self as well as experience feelings is limited even in cases where the treatment remains viable (Abend, Porder, & Willick, 1983). The patient may have such intense feelings about the analyst that he cannot recognize their inappropriateness.

Beneficial psychical change may occur irrespective of the theoretical stance of the psychoanalyst. This has reinforced the charge that analytic treatment is a process of suggestion over an extended period of time (Grunbaum, 1984). This criticism has not been withdrawn, despite the clear connection that exists between suggestibility and the state of the patient–analyst relationship (transference). Is the analysis of the transference sufficient to control patients' suggestibility? A free discussion of the role of suggestion in the psychoanalytic process has a positive side. It may alert analysts to the danger of unwittingly exploiting patients' suggestibility when the analyst's input to the treatment process is given priority. Enhancing suggestibility is synonymous with infantilizing the patient. This runs counter to the aim of psychoanalytic treatment, which is to enable the patient to recover his lost independence. This aim will be furthered if the analyst's contributions are limited to sweeping away the obstacles (transference, ego, and superego resistances) that prevent the patient from giving expression to his wishes, fears, phantasies, and memories. This restores the continuity between the patient's present and past mental life— a continuity that has been lost.

CHAPTER ELEVEN

Is there a way forward?

The purpose of this book has been to show that Freud's introduction of the theory of the death instinct and the "structural" formulations laid the foundation for the theories of contemporary psychoanalysis. The concept of the death instinct marked a change in Freud's thinking. He no longer found it necessary to anchor this concept in clinical observations, as had been his practice in the past. He used the new concept to reinterpret clinical facts. He was untroubled by his realization that the "structural" theory was a reformulation of what had already been observed. Freud (1920g, 1940a) reconciled his new ideas with his earlier metapsychology. Nevertheless, the effect was to cause the original ideas to slip into the background (Yorke, 1993, 1995, 1996).

Today psychoanalytic theories and techniques of treatment are challenged. Basic descriptive and explanatory concepts (e.g. resistance and repression) are subject to criticism. Even the method of free association has come under attack (Grunbaum, 1984). This makes it essential for psychoanalysts to acknowledge the provisional nature of their theories. Explanatory concepts must be subject to scrutiny in order to confirm or deny their validity. This may be unimportant to some analysts and to the hermeneutists, but, as Steiner (1995) warns, the too-free interpretation of the narrative constructed by patient and analyst may lead to the risk of a "... sort of psychoanalysis à la carte, where anything goes" (Steiner, 1995). As Roiphe (1995) declares, verification is a necessary step if psychoanalysis is to achieve the status of a scientific discipline. An objective approach is taken seriously by many psychoanalysts. This as is attested by the collection of papers published by *The Journal of the American Psychoanalytic Association* (1995) under the heading of "Psychoanalysis as Science".

There is little agreement amongst psychoanalysts about how the analytic situation may be employed to verify psychoanalytic facts. Some favour the recording of data in order to build up a database of analytic work (Roiphe, 1995; Spence, 1994). Data of this kind might provide the raw material for hypotheses that could be tested (Edelson, 1984; Spence, 1994). Others are critical of this methodology, claiming that it provides a spurious objectivity. Reliance, in this view (O'Shaughnessy, 1994; Tuckett, 1994), should be placed on the analyst's integrity and thoroughness of his own analysis to counter the subjective influences of the patient–analyst situation. By a careful evaluation of sessional material it should be possible to verify, successfully, psychoanalytic facts.

Unconvinced by this argument and mindful of the problems connected with research confined to the analytic situation, analysts have looked for alternative forms and methods of research. These methods have been conducted apart from the analytic situation while making use of psychoanalytic knowledge. Illustrative of this is the work of Shevrin (1988) with mainly neurotic patients. Patients' brain potentials were recorded while they were being presented with supraliminal and subliminal stimuli which consisted of psychoanalytic formulations derived from an assessment of the patient's psychopathology.

Criticism that clinical facts alone cannot validate psychoanalytic assumptions applies equally to observations made on patients who are not undergoing psychoanalytic treatment and on those who are. It is argued that clinical observations, which are ostensibly reported to verify a psychoanalytic hypothesis, must be regarded with suspicion, because they are merely additions to lists of selected positive examples. They are dismissed as anecdotal. This criticism effectively excludes the contribution of those clinicians (Frosch, 1983) who use psychoanalytic concepts in their work with patients suffering from schizophrenic psychoses or organic mental states. The result is that categories of clinical facts are denied consideration. However, these clinical facts have their own validity by virtue of their recurrent character and identical form and content. They are relevant for a number of psychoanalytic assumptions. One of fundamental importance is the theory underlying the method of free association. It was Freud's (1896b, 1900a) experience in the neuroses and dreams that "when conscious purposive ideas are abandoned, concealed purposive ideas assume control of the current of ideas, and that superficial associations are only substitutes by displacement for suppressed deeper ones" (Freud, 1900a). Critics of the method of free association claim that the stream of involuntary thoughts that comes to the patient's mind is haphazard and arbitrarily chosen. The analyst exploits chance connections to fabricate his interpretations.

The substitution by displacement of unconscious thoughts in favour of "superficial" ideas may be observed directly during acute psychotic attacks and in long-standing cases of hebephrenic–catatonic schizophrenia. The mental state of these patients may be compared to the neurotic patient who free-associates. The voluntary control of thought is lost in the former and temporarily given up in the latter. In both categories "superficial" and apparently disconnected thoughts conceal ideas that would evoke distressing affects.

> A 37-year-old married woman suffered from hypomania. The manic attack followed the discovery that her husband was unfaithful. In the course of an interview her attention was constantly seized by the floral design of the carpet. Names of flowers repeatedly interrupted her train of thought. This gave it an unintelligible quality. The name "Rose" was particularly conspicuous. This was the name of the husband's lover. In this instance, what appeared to be aimless, involuntary thoughts were determined by unconscious purposive ideas. When confronted by the connection, the patient's elated and excited state was replaced by tears and depression of mood.

A further example is provided in the case of a man who suffered from a non-remitting (hebephrenic–catatonic) schizophrenia. He shared a locked ward at night with some disturbed and potentially violent patients. He was very afraid of them. When with the author in the hospital library, he asked whether he could have scars on his wrist (caused by a suicidal attempt) removed by plastic surgery. Suddenly this subject was interrupted by what seemed to be disconnected associations— mainly thoughts about Robert Louis Stevenson's novel *Treasure Island* and the character "Ben Gunn". He followed this with the name "Robinson". The connection between his thoughts became clear to the author when he realized that while the patient was talking about his scars, a man who shared the patient's ward entered the room. The author knew that the man's name was Gunn. The patient's conscious thoughts were determined by unconscious purposive ideas—namely that he, like Ben Gunn and Robinson Crusoe, was marooned and surrounded by unpredictable aggressive savages (the patients in the ward).

The current emphasis on hypothesis-testing research has devalued the contributions that exploratory studies can make to verifying Freud's theory of the mental apparatus (Freud, 1900a). An opportunity to support this verification is afforded by patients suffering from non-remitting schizophrenias and organic mental states. The speech content of these patients, as the last example illustrates, reveals that they assimilate extraneous percepts without being conscious of so doing. This makes their speech unintelligible and inappropriate. These assimilated impressions consist of some aspect of the psychiatrist's appearance and behaviour, or some detail of the room in which the meeting is taking place (Freeman, 1969). Bleuler (1911) described this phenomenon as it occurs in the schizophrenias as "a peculiar kind of distractibility". There is a defect of selective attention.

These clinical observations have been paralleled by experimental investigations. These show that there are stages in the perceptual process during which the memory traces of visual stimuli pass through a series of transformations before they become conscious as images of visual percepts (Fisher, 1963; G. S. Klein, 1959). A distinction is drawn (G. S. Klein, 1959) between the registration of perceptual data—occurring outside consciousness—and consciousness of percepts. Klein has suggested that registration of external stimuli in the healthy occurs on a wider and more indiscriminate scale than could ever have been imagined. There must, therefore, be inhibitory mechanisms that govern the fate of these mental registrations. It may be hypothesized (Poetzl, 1917) that these inhibitory influences have been subject to dissolution in hebephrenic–catatonic schizophrenia and in organic mental states. In Freud's (1900a) description of his hypothetical mental apparatus, percepts do not make an instantaneous appearance in consciousness. They first pass through an unconscious phase. They are registered, as Klein (1959) has shown, outside consciousness. For a percept to become conscious, it must first become the focus of attention. This is unlikely to happen in the mentally healthy if the percept has the potential to evoke distressing affects. A fruitful field of research lies in a systematic enquiry into the distractibility of psychotic patients. Chapman and McGhie (1962) identified a defect of selective attention in hebephrenic–catatonic schizophrenic patients. A suitably designed study could confirm or refute the theory that affects may interfere with the function of selective attention—a function Freud (1900a) allocated to the system Perceptual–Conscious.

Chapter 1 investigated the subject of the ubiquity of wishing in the healthy and the mentally ill. In dreams and in the content of delusions, substitution occurs on an extensive scale. An idea, a word, a person, is substituted for another idea, word, or person. This is seen clearly in organic mental states.

An elderly man who suffered from arteriosclerotic dementia denied that he was in hospital. He insisted that he was living on his farm, as he had done all his life. He pointed to the trees and hedges in the hospital grounds to prove his point. He misidentified male doctors and nurses as his brothers or fellow farm-workers. From time to time he would ask the author: "What's your work?" but forgot as soon as he was told. One day when talking about a sick cow on the farm, he asked: "Are you a vegetarian, a victorian?" The words "vegetarian" and "victorian" were as near as he could get to a "veterinarian", which substituted for the word "doctor". At other times he would spontaneously refer to the author as "doctor". This indicated that the fault lay in voluntary recall and not in the memory trace of the word "doctor". Everything was determined by wish-fulfilment—the substitution of veterinarian for doctor allowed the thought that he was back on his farm.

Expressions of wishes fulfilled are commonplace in chronic brain syndrome (Alzheimer's disease, arteriosclerotic dementia, epilepsy, etc.). As in the case quoted, psychically fulfilled wishes are most strikingly shown in misidentifications and misperceptions. It is only in a small number of cases that delusions and hallucinations with a persecutory content occur. Frequently these "persecutory" experiences are a response to a failure to understand the patient's needs and situation. They are, rather, a reaction having origins in endopsychic sources. Where actual persecutory delusions occur, they can be traced to anxiety arising from psychically fulfilled wishes (Yorke et al., 1989).

These data are important because they trench on a recurring problem for psychoanalysis. Too often psychoanalysts fail to acknowledge a tendency to impose theoretical ideas on the empirical data. Are the clinical facts of chronic brain syndrome simply the result of psychical dissolution, allowing the exposure of wishes psychically fulfilled? Another theory is that psychically fulfilled wishes result from omnipotent reparative phantasies that remove the destructive attacks on objects and free the individual from persecution. These theories are diametrically opposite to one another—wish-fulfilment is primary in the one and secondary in the other. Adherence to one or other theory is not synonymous with verification (Spence, 1994).

The relevance for psychoanalysis of the misidentifications that occur in chronic brain syndrome lies in the observation that these patients present *ad oculos* what may only be inferred from neurotic patients' utterances and behaviour during psychoanalytic treatment. In both groups of patients—the organically damaged and the neurotically afflicted—there are "false connections" (Freud with Breuer, 1895d). In the former, the "false connections" result from wishes fulfilled, in the latter, it is the analytic setting that induces a temporal regression (Freud, 1900a).

The clinical facts described here provide a practical and theoretical perspective from which to view Freud's (1900a) concept of a mental apparatus. The phenomena suggest that wishing, as a mental derivative of instinct, acts as the driving force of mental life. The translation of wishes into conscious intentions and actions is dependent on the operation of the pleasure principle (see Chapter 1). While wishes represent impulses (unconscious mental processes) arising within the apparatus, percepts constitute the stimuli impinging upon the apparatus from the environment. The clinical facts of mental pathology lead to the hypothesis that internal and external stimuli can only reach consciousness if they do not evoke unpleasure (see Chapter 1).

There is another field of clinical research that has had unexpected implications for psychoanalysis (Solms, 1993, 1995). Solms' clinico-pathological studies on brain-damaged patients were primarily concerned with the "neurological organization of dreaming" (Solms, 1993). Secondarily, their relevance for Freud's (1900a) theory of dreams became apparent. Briefly, Solms observed that dreaming stopped when there were lesions of the inferior parietal and deep frontal areas. There was non-visual dreaming with medial occipito-temporal lesions. Dreaming was preserved with brain stem core lesions. Limbic lesions led to patients being unable to distinguish dreams from reality. Complex-partial (temporal lobe) epilepsy was associated with recurrent stereotypical nightmares.

On the basis of his neuropsychological findings, Solms (1997) concluded that forebrain structures are essential for dreaming. Anything that disturbs sleep can initiate a dream. In dreaming there is a retrogressive movement affecting "the scene of action of mental life" (Freud, 1900a). This regression from the dorso-lateral frontal region, which is the executive agent of normal waking cognition, moves towards the parieto-occipital systems—"Nocturnal mentation is thus deprived of the characteristic goal directiveness of waking mental life and the activating impulse is worked over symbolically in visuo-spatial consciousness" (Solms, 1995). This is akin to Freud's (1900a) concept of topographic regression proposed to explain the hallucinatory quality of the dream. Solms' studies on the nature of the dream throw light on a problem that troubled Freud (1900a). He was not satisfied that the formal characteristics of the dream could be accounted for by the processes of the dream work that converted the latent dream thoughts into the manifest content. Solms' research (1995, 1997) appears to fulfil Freud's (1900a) requirement that "the findings of other enquiries" (Freud, 1900a) are necessary to solve the problem of the dream.

It is reassuring and encouraging for analysts to read about the work of other scientific disciplines that support a particular psychoanalytic theory. However, there are times when this knowledge challenges an accepted psychoanalytic concept. An instance of this is the anatomical record of the infant's developing dentition. This has important implications for the concept of oral sadism (Freeman & Freeman, 1992). Abraham (see Chapter 7) stated that oral–sadistic wish phantasies come into play as mental representations only when the infant's teeth erupt and the muscles of mastication reach their full development. Klein (1932, 1935) revised the date of the origin of these oral–sadistic phantasies, *claiming that they were active from birth*. The anatomical record shows that from birth until the 6th to 9th month of life the infant is incapable of biting or chewing. The Kleinian position is that the oral–sadistic phantasies are innate and constitutionally determined, hence their independence from somatic developmental processes. Abraham's (1924) theory is closer to the empirical data.

The research that has been conducted inside and outside the analytic situation reflects the conviction of many psychoanalysts that there is a way forward for psychoanalysis as a subject conforming to scientific criteria. If these researches are successful, some theories and explanatory concepts may have to be jettisoned. There is, as Roiphe (1995) reminds her readers, ". . . an historical trend of hostility towards empirical research by psychoanalysts". This hostility springs from the fear that research will destroy what is most valuable in the patient–analyst encounter. In this view the analytic situation is considered inviolable. It must be free from the constraints that empirical research imposes. Those who subscribe to this approach—and this includes the hermeneutists—do not think it necessary to take account of the influence suggestibility may have on their interpretations and on the patient's reactions.

That strict analysis of the transference and countertransference reactions will bring suggestibility under control has yet to be substantiated. As long as a theory such as this and other psychoanalytic facts are denied investigation, the charge that psychoanalysis is a long-drawn-out process of suggestion will remain.

It is fitting to end this book, which follows Freud's (1900a, 1915c, 1915d, 1915e, 1917d) evolutionary theory of mind, with a brief reference to a field of enquiry that seems distant from the psychoanalytic situation. It is the ethological observations that have been made on chimpanzees (Holmstrom, 1991). Striking signs of an oedipal constellation are to be observed in these creatures, whose genetic endowment is nearest to man. These studies are impressive because they reveal the early phylogenetic antecedents of contemporary man's personality and of his social organization. In their daily work, psychoanalysts are offered the opportunity to observe the remains of that archaic heritage in their analysis of dreams. In Chapter 1 examples are given of how dream analysis reveals the presence of a primitive cognition. This is expressed in the means whereby (latent) dream thoughts find representation (Freud, 1900a). The dissolution that affects the psychical life of some schizophrenic patients (particularly the hebephrenic–catatonic type) also "releases a similar paralogic" thinking (Arieti, 1955). As Freud (1900a) writes: "Dreams and neuroses seem to have preserved more mental antiquities than we could have imagined possible; so that psychoanalysis may claim a high place amongst the sciences which are concerned with the reconstruction of the earliest and most obscure periods of the beginnings of the human race."

A note on child psychoanalysis

R eaders of this book will have discerned from the accounts of psychoanalytic theories of development that the analysis of mentally disturbed children has led, as in the case of adult patients, to the description of many psychoanalytic clinical facts. There is no dispute about the clinical facts in the individual case as with anxiety symptoms, separation fears, disturbances of sleep, appetite, and excretion. Again, it is the psychoanalytic facts that cause the problem. They are inevitably connected to the analyst's preferred theory of psychopathogenesis and technique of treatment. The divergence in the content of psychoanalytic facts is to be found in the respective theories of Anna Freud (1965) and Melanie Klein (1940, 1957).

The child analyst's position with regard to the verification of psychoanalytic clinical facts is no different from that in the analysis of adult patients. In the case of rescue phantasies, for example, which children may enact during treatment, different explanations of the phenomenon result in different technical interventions (interpretations). This compounds the problem of verification. Rescue phantasies were regarded by Freud (1910h) as derivatives of the

Oedipus complex. Having renounced much of the emotional ego-centrism (A. Freud, 1965), the child may perceive the mother, separate from himself, and as a person with her own needs. The core of the rescue phantasy consists of the unconscious wish to supplant the father (be the father) and give the mother a child (Freud, 1909c, 1910h). This unconscious phantasy will only be brought to the child's attention if it is playing an important part in the causation of a symptom or in aberrant behaviour.

The Kleinian understanding of a rescue phantasy is different while it, too, acknowledges the oedipal colouring. A rescue phantasy springs from the depressive position in which the child finds himself. Depressive anxieties have arisen because the child fears that his envy and acquisitive greed (Klein, 1957) have damaged the mother. The rescue phantasy is a psychical act of omnipotent reparation. The mother is restored. This requires that the depressive anxieties have to be interpreted mainly through the medium of the transference. There is in both approaches a confluence of the child's contribution (the rescue phantasy) on the one side and the analyst's contribution (the interpretations based on one or other unconscious phantasy) on the other. This complicates the matter of verification. It remains as elusive as in the case of adult patients.

Little light has been thrown on the validity of psychoanalytic facts found in child analysis by recent observational research on infants (Emde, 1983; Stern, 1985). It is sufficient here to quote Yorke (1993) on the developmental theories of Emde (1983) and Stern (1985). Yorke (1993) writes: "The empirical data from the research under scrutiny do not establish that infants possess a self or are capable of self/other differentiation in a psychoanalytic sense. Statements about the intra-psychical experiences of infants are theoretical postulates, not empirical generalisations or meta-phors."

REFERENCES

Abend, S. M., Porder, M. S., & Willick, M. S. (1983). *Borderline Patients: Psychoanalytic Perspectives*. New York: International Universities Press.

Abraham, K. (1908). Psychosexual differences between hysteria and dementia praecox. In: *Selected Papers on Psychoanalysis*. London: Hogarth, 1942 [reprinted London: Karnac Books, 1988].

Abraham, K. (1915). *A Psychoanalytic Dialogue: The Letters of Sigmund Freud and Karl Abraham*. London: Hogarth, 1965.

Abraham, K. (1916). The first pregenital stage of the libido. In: *Selected Papers on Psychoanalysis*. London: Hogarth, 1942 [reprinted London: Karnac Books, 1988].

Abraham, K. (1919). A particular form of neurotic resistance against the psychoanalytic method. In: *Selected Papers on Psychoanalysis*. London: Hogarth, 1942 [reprinted London: Karnac Books, 1988].

Abraham, K. (1924). A short study of the development of the libido in the light of mental disorders. In: *Selected Papers on Psychoanalysis*. London: Hogarth, 1942 [reprinted London: Karnac Books, 1988].

Abrams, S. (1994). The publication of clinical facts. *International Journal of Psycho-Analysis, 75*: 1201–1212.

Arieti, S. (1955). *Interpretation of Schizophrenia*. New York: Brunner.

Arlow, J., & Brenner, C. (1969). The psychopathology of the psychoses. *International Journal of Psycho-Analysis, 50*: 5–14.

Baker, R. (1993). The patient's discovery of the psychoanalyst as a new object. *International Journal of Psycho-Analysis, 74*: 1223–1233.

Balint, M. (1935). Critical notes on the pregenital organisations of the libido. In: *Primary Love and Psychoanalytic Technique*. London: Hogarth, 1952 [reprinted London: Karnac Books, 1985].

Balint, M. (1952). *Primary Love and Psychoanalytic Technique*. London: Hogarth, 1952 [reprinted London: Karnac Books, 1985].

Balint, M. (1968). *The Basic Fault*. London: Tavistock.

Bernard, C. (1867). The internal environment. In: *Claude Bernard, Physiologist, J.M.D. Ormstead*. London: Cassel, 1939.

Bibring, E. (1953). The mechanism of depression. In: P. Greenacre (Ed.), *Affective Disorders*. New York: International Universities Press.

Bion, W. R. (1959). Attacks on linking. *International Journal of Psycho-Analysis, 40*: 305–315. [Also in: *Second Thoughts: Selected Papers on Psychoanalysis*. London: Heinemann, 1967. Reprinted London: Karnac Books, 1987.]

Bion, W. R. (1962). A theory of thinking. *International Journal of Psycho-Analysis, 43*: 306–310. [Also in: *Second Thoughts: Selected Papers on Psychoanalysis*. London: Heinemann, 1967. Reprinted London: Karnac Books, 1987.]

Bleuler, E. (1911). *Dementia Praecox or The Group of Schizophrenias*. New York: International Universities Press, 1955.

Bleuler, M. (1978). *The Schizophrenic Disorders*. London: Yale University Press.

Bollas, C. (1979). The transformational object. *International Journal of Psycho-Analysis, 60*: 97–107.

Breuer, J. (1895a). Fräulein Anna O. In: S. Freud & J. Breuer, *Studies on Hysteria* (pp. 21–47). *S.E.*, 2.

Breuer, J. (1895b). Theoretical. In: S. Freud & J. Breuer, *Studies on Hysteria* (pp. 183–252). *S.E.*, 2.

Caper, R. (1994). What is a clinical fact? *International Journal of Psycho-Analysis, 75*: 903–913.

Chapman, J., & McGhie, A. (1962). A comparative study of disordered attention in schizophrenia. *Journal of Mental Science, 108*: 455–487.

Chertok, L., & Stengers, I. (1992). *A Critique of Psychoanalytic Reason*. Stanford, CA: Stanford University Press.

Couch, A. (1989). Extra-transference interpretations: a defence of classical technique (unpublished).

Couch, A. (1995). Anna Freud's adult psychoanalytic technique: a defence of classical analysis. *International Journal of Psycho-Analysis, 76*: 153–171.

Critchley, M. (1953). *The Parietal Lobes.* London: Arnold.

Edelson, M. (1984). *Hypothesis and Evidence in Psychoanalysis.* Chicago, IL: University of Chicago Press.

Emde, R. N. (1983). The prerepresentational self and its affective care. *Psychoanalytic Study of the Child, 38*: 165–192

Ey, H. (1969). Outline of an organo-dynamic conception of the structure, nosography and pathogenesis of mental diseases. In: E. Strauss (Ed.), *Psychiatry and Philosophy.* New York: Springer.

Fairbairn, W. R. D. (1940). Schizoid factors in the personality. In: *Psychoanalytic Studies of the Personality.* London: Routledge and Kegan Paul, 1952.

Fairbairn, W. R. D. (1944). Endopsychic structures considered in terms of object relations. In: *Psychoanalytic Studies of the Personality.* London: Routledge and Kegan Paul, 1952.

Fairbairn, W. R. D. (1958). On the nature and aims of psychoanalysis. *International Journal of Psycho-Analysis, 39*: 374–385.

Federn, P. (1953). *Ego Psychology and the Psychoses.* London: Imago [reprinted London: Karnac Books, 1977].

Feldman, M. (1997). Projective identification: the analyst's involvement. *International Journal of Psycho-Analysis, 78*: 227–241.

Fenichel, O. (1941). *Problems of Psychoanalytic Technique.* New York: Psychoanalytic Quarterly.

Ferenczi, S. (1912). On the part played by homosexuality in the pathogenesis of paranoia. In: *Sex and Psychoanalysis.* Boston: Badger, 1916. Also in: *First Contributions to Psychoanalysis.* (pp. 154–186). London: Hogarth Press, 1952 [reprinted London: Karnac Books, 1994].

Ferenczi, S. (1928). The elasticity of psychoanalytic technique. In: *Final Contributions to the Problems and Methods of Psychoanalysis.* New York: Basic Books, 1955 [reprinted London: Karnac Books, 1994].

Ferenczi, S., & Rank, O. (1925). *The Development of Psychoanalysis.* New York: International Universities Press, 1986.

Fisher, C. (1963). Studies on the psychopathology of sleep and dreams. *American Journal of Psychiatry, 119*: 1160–1172.

Freeman, R. E., & Freeman, T. (1992). An anatomical commentary on the concept of infantile oral sadism. *International Journal of Psycho-Analysis, 73*: 343–348.

Freeman, R. E., & Kells, B. (1996). A dysmorphophobic reaction to cosmetic dentistry: observations and responses to psychotherapeutic interventions. *Psychoanalytic Psychotherapy, 10*: 21–31.

Freeman, T. (1951). Pregnancy as a precipitant of mental illness in men. *British Journal of Medical Psychology, 24*: 56–63.

Freeman, T. (1962a). Narcissism and defensive processes in schizophrenic states. *International Journal of Psycho-Analysis, 43*: 415–425.

Freeman, T. (1962b). The psychoanalytic observation of chronic schizophrenic reactions. In: D. Richter et al. (Eds.), *Aspects of Psychiatric Research*. London: Oxford University Press.

Freeman, T. (1964). Some aspects of pathological narcissism. *Journal of the American Psychoanalytical Association, 12*: 540–561.

Freeman, T. (1965). *Studies on Psychosis*. London: Tavistock.

Freeman, T. (1969). *The Psychopathology of the Psychoses*. London: Tavistock.

Freeman, T. (1970). The psychopathology of the psychoses: a reply to Arlow and Brenner. *International Journal of Psycho-Analysis, 51*: 407–425.

Freeman, T. (1973). *A Psychoanalytic Study of the Psychoses*. New York: International Universities Press.

Freeman, T. (1976). *Childhood Psychopathology and Adult Psychoses*. New York: International Universities Press.

Freeman, T. (1984). Erotomania and transference love. *Psychopathology and Psychotherapy, 1*: 19–29.

Freeman, T. (1988). *The Psychoanalyst in Psychiatry*. London: Karnac Books.

Freeman, T. (1990). Psychoanalytic aspects of morbid jealousy in women. *British Journal of Psychiatry, 156*: 68–72.

Freeman, T., Cameron, J. L., & McGhie, A. (1958). *Chronic Schizophrenia*. London: Tavistock.

Freeman, T., & Gathercole, C. E. (1966). Perseveration—the clinical symptoms in chronic schizophrenia and organic dementia. *British Journal of Psychiatry, 112*: 27–32.

Freud, A. (1936). *The Ego and the Mechanisms of Defence*. London: Hogarth [reprinted London: Karnac Books, 1993].

Freud, A. (1954). The widening scope of indications for psychoanalysis. *Journal of the American Psychoanalytical Association*, 2: 96–102.

Freud, A. (1965). *Normality and Pathology in Childhood*. London: Pen-
guin [reprinted London: Karnac Books, 1989].

Freud, S. (1891b). *On Aphasia*. London, Imago, 1953.

Freud, S., with J. Breuer (1893a). On the psychical mechanism of hysterical phenomena: preliminary communication. *S.E.*, 2. London:
Hogarth.

Freud, S. (1893f). Charcot. *S.E.*, 3.

Freud, S. (1894a). The neuro-psychoses of defence. *S.E.*, 3.

Freud, S. (1895b). On the grounds for detaching a particular syndrome
from neurasthenia under the description of anxiety neurosis. *S.E.*,
3.

Freud, S., with J. Breuer (1895d). Studies on Hysteria. *S.E.*, 2.

Freud, S. (1896b). Further remarks on the neuro-psychoses of defence.
S.E., 3.

Freud, S. (1896c). The aetiology of hysteria. *S.E.*, 3.

Freud, S. (1898a). Sexuality in the aetiology of the neuroses. *S.E.*, 3.

Freud, S. (1900a). *The Interpretation of Dreams. S.E.*, 4–5.

Freud, S. (1905d). *Three Essays on the Theory of Sexuality. S.E.*, 7.

Freud, S. (1909c). Family Romances. *S.E.*, 9.

Freud, S. (1910c). *Leonardo da Vinci and a Memory of his Childhood. S.E.*,
11.

Freud, S. (1910h). A special type of object choice made by men. *S.E.*, 11.

Freud, S. (1911b). Formulations on the two principles of mental functioning. *S.E.*, 12.

Freud, S. (1911c). Psychoanalytic notes on an autobiographical account of a case of paranoia. *S.E.*, 12.

Freud, S. (1914c). On narcissism, an introduction. *S.E.*, 16.

Freud, S. (1915c). Instincts and their vicissitudes. *S.E.*, 14.

Freud, S. (1915d). Repression. *S.E.*, 14.

Freud, S. (1915e). The Unconscious. *S.E.*, 14.

Freud, S. (1916–17). *Introductory Lectures on Psycho-Analysis. S.E.*, 16.

Freud, S. (1917d). Metapsychological supplement to the theory of
dreams. *S.E.*, 14.

Freud, S. (1917e). Mourning and melancholia. *S.E.*, 14.

Freud, S. (1918b). From the history of an infantile neurosis. *S.E.*, 17.

Freud, S. (1919a). Lines of advance in psychoanalytic theory. *S.E.*, 17.

Freud, S. (1920g). *Beyond the Pleasure Principle. S.E., 18.*

Freud, S. (1921c). *Group Psychology and the Analysis of the Ego. S.E., 18.*

Freud, S. (1923b). *The Ego and the Id. S.E., 19.*

Freud, S. (1924c). The economic problem of masochism. *S.E., 19.*

Freud, S. (1926d). Inhibitions, symptoms and anxiety. *S.E., 20.*

Freud, S. (1933a). *New Introductory Lectures on Psychoanalysis. SE., 22.*

Freud, S. (1937c). Analysis terminable and interminable. *S.E., 23.*

Freud, S. (1940a). *An Outline of Psychoanalysis. S.E., 23.*

Freud, S. (1940e). Splitting of the ego in the process of defence. *S.E., 23.*

Fromm-Reichmann, F. (1941). Notes on the development and treatment of schizophrenics by psychoanalytic psychotherapy. *Psychiatry, 11:* 263–274.

Frosch, J. (1983). *The Psychotic Process.* New York: International Universities Press.

Glover, E. (1949). *Psychoanalysis.* London: Staples Press.

Glover, E. (1955). *The Technique of Psychoanalysis.* London: Baillière, Tindall and Cox.

Goldstein, K. (1943). Concerning rigidity, character and personality. *Character and Personality, 11:* 209–226.

Greenson, R. (1985). *The Technique and Practice of Psychoanalysis.* London: Hogarth.

Grotstein, J. (1977a). The psychoanalytic concept of schizophrenia: the dilemma. *International Journal of Psycho-Analysis, 58:* 403–426.

Grotstein, J. (1977b). The psychoanalytic concept of schizophrenia: the reconciliation. *International Journal of Psycho-Analysis, 58:* 447–452.

Grunbaum, A. (1984). *The Foundations of Psychoanalysis.* Berkeley, CA: University of California Press.

Habermas, J. (1971). *Knowledge and Human Interest.* Boston: Beacon Press.

Heimann, P. (1950). On countertransference. *International Journal of Psycho-Analysis, 31:* 56–60.

Heimann, P. (1960). Countertransference. *British Journal of Medical Psychology, 33:* 37–50.

Holmstrom, R. (1991). On the phylogeny of the Oedipus complex: psychoanalytic aspects of the ethology of anthropoid apes. *Psychoanalysis and Contemporary Thought, 14:* 271–315.

Holt, R. R. (1981). The death and transfiguration of metapsychology. *International Journal of Psycho-Analysis, 8:* 129–143.

Jackson, J. H. (1884). Remarks on evolution and dissolution of the nervous system. *Journal of Mental Science, 33*: 25–48.

Janet, P. (1893). Quelques definitions récentes de l'hysterie. *Archives of Neurology, 25*: 407–415.

Joseph, B. (1983). On understanding and not understanding. *International Journal of Psycho-Analysis, 64*: 291–298.

Katan, M. (1954). The importance of the non-psychotic part of the personality in schizophrenia. *International Journal of Psycho-Analysis, 35*: 119–125.

Katan, M. (1979). Further explorations of the schizophrenic regression to the undifferentiated state: a study of the assessment of the unconscious. *International Journal of Psycho-Analysis, 60*: 145–175.

Kernberg, O. (1984). *Personality disorders*. New Haven, CT: Yale University Press.

Klauber, J. (1976). *Elements of the Psychoanalytic Relationship and their Therapeutic Implications in Difficulties in the Analytic Encounter*. London: Tavistock, 1981.

Klein, G. S. (1959). Consciousness in psychoanalytic theory—some implications for current research in perception. *Journal of the American Psychoanalytical Association, 7*: 5–20.

Klein, M. (1932). *The Psychoanalysis of Children*. London: Hogarth [reprinted London: Karnac Books, 1998].

Klein, M. (1935). A contribution to the psychogenesis of manic-depressive states. In: *The Writings of Melanie Klein, 1*. London: Hogarth, 1975 [reprinted London: Karnac Books, 1992].

Klein, M. (1940). Mourning and its relation to manic-depressive states. In: *The Writings of Melanie Klein, 1*. London: Hogarth [reprinted London: Karnac Books, 1992].

Klein, M. (1946). Notes on some schizoid mechanisms. In: *The Writings of Melanie Klein, 2*. London: Hogarth [reprinted London: Karnac Books, 1975].

Klein, M. (1957). Envy and gratitude. In: *The Writings of Melanie Klein, 3*. London: Hogarth [reprinted London: Karnac Books, 1993].

Knight, G. (1953). Management and psychotherapy of the borderline patient. *Bulletin of the Menninger Clinic, 17*: 139–150.

Kohon, G. (1986). Countertransference: an independent view. In: G. Kohon (Ed.), *The British School of Psychoanalysis: The Independent Tradition*. London: Free Association Books, 1986.

Kohut, H. (1971). *The Analysis of the Self.* New York: International Universities Press.

Kohut, H. (1977). *The Restoration of the Self.* New York: International Universities Press.

Kretchmer, E. (1918). *The Sensitive Delusion of Reference.* Berlin: Springer.

London, N. (1973). An essay on psychoanalytic theory: two theories of schizophrenia. *International Journal of Psycho-Analysis, 54*: 169–194.

Lucas, R. (1985). Contribution of psychoanalysis to the management of psychotic patients. *Psychoanalytic Psychotherapy, 1*: 3–17.

Luria, A. R. (1965). Two kinds of motor perseveration in massive injury of the frontal lobes. *Brain, 88*: 1–10.

Milton, J. (1658). "Methought I saw. . . ." In: *Milton.* London: Nonesuch Press, 1960.

Nunberg, H. (1955). *Principles of Psychoanalysis.* New York: International Universities Press.

Ogden, T. H. (1980). On the nature of schizophrenic conflict. *International Journal of Psycho-Analysis, 61*: 513–534.

Orenstein, A., & Orenstein, P. (1994). On the conceptualisation of clinical facts in psychoanalysis. *International Journal of Psycho-Analysis, 75*: 977–994.

O'Shaughnessy, E. (1994). What is a clinical fact? *International Journal of Psycho-Analysis, 75*: 939–947.

Pao, P. N. (1979). *Schizophrenic Disorders.* New York: International Universities Press.

Payne, R. W. (1961). Cognitive abnormalities. In: H. Eysenck (Ed.), *Handbook of Abnormal Psychology.* New York: Basic Books.

Poetzl, O. (1917). The relationship between experimentally induced dream images and indirect vision. In: *Preconscious Stimulation in Dreams, Associations and Images. Psychological Issues (Monograph 7).* New York: International Universities Press.

Pruyser, P. (1975). What splits in splitting? *Bulletin of the Menniger Clinic, 39*: 1–46.

Psychoanalysis as science (1995). *Journal of the American Psychoanalytical Association, 43*: 963–1049.

Reich, A. (1951). On countertransference. *International Journal of Psycho-Analysis, 32*: 25–31.

Reisenberg-Malcolm, R. (1994). Conceptualisation of clinical facts in the analytic process. *International Journal of Psycho-Analysis, 75*: 1031–1040.

Reik, T. (1936). *Ritual*. London: Hogarth.

Ricoeur, P. (1977). The question of proof in Freud's psychoanalytic writing. *Journal of the American Psychoanalytic Association, 25*: 835–871.

Roiphe, J. (1995). The conceptualisation and communication of clinical facts. *International Journal of Psycho-Analysis, 76*: 1179–1190.

Rosenfeld, H. (1950). Notes on the psychopathology of confusional states in chronic schizophrenia. *International Journal of Psycho-Analysis, 31*: 132–137.

Rosenfeld, H. (1952). Notes on the psychoanalysis of the superego conflict in an acute schizophrenic patient. *International Journal of Psycho-Analysis, 33*: 111–131.

Rosenfeld, H. (1954). Considerations regarding the psychoanalytic approach to acute and chronic schizophrenia. In: *Psychotic States*. London: Hogarth, 1965 [reprinted London: Karnac Books, 1990].

Rosenfeld, H. (1964). On the psychopathology of narcissism: a clinical approach. *International Journal of Psycho-Analysis, 45*: 332–337.

Rosenfeld, H. (1971). A clinical approach to the psychoanalytic theory of the life and death instincts: an investigation into the aggressive aspects of narcissism. *International Journal of Psycho-Analysis, 52*: 169–178.

Rosenfeld, H. (1987). *Impasse and Interpretation*. London: Tavistock/ Routledge.

Sandler, A. M., & Sandler, J. (1994). Comments on the conceptualisation of clinical facts in psychoanalysis. *International Journal of Psycho-Analysis, 75*: 995–1010.

Sandler, J. (1992). Reflections on developments in the theory of psychoanalytic technique. *International Journal of Psycho-Analysis, 73*: 109–198.

Sandler, J. (1997). The psychoanalytic theory of repression and the unconscious. In: J. Sandler & P. Fonagy (Eds.), *Recovered Memories of Abuse: True or False?* London: Karnac Books.

Schafer, R. (1994). The conceptualization of clinical facts. *International Journal of Psychoanalysis, 75*: 1023–1030.

Schilder, P. (1953). *Medical Psychology*. New York: International Universities Press.

Schimek, J. G. (1975). The interpretation of the past: childhood trauma, psychical reality and historical truth. *Journal of the American Psychoanalytical Association, 23*: 845–965.

Searles, H. (1963). Transference psychosis in the psychotherapy of chronic schizophrenia. *International Journal of Psycho-Analysis, 44*: 249–281.

Segal, H. (1956). Depression in the schizophrenic. *International Journal of Psycho-Analysis, 37*: 339–343.

Shevrin, H. (1988). Unconscious conflict: a convergent psychodynamic and electrophysiological approach. In: M. J. Horowitz (Ed.), *Psychodynamics and Cognition*. Chicago, IL: University of Chicago Press.

Solms, M. (1993). Summary and discussion of the paper: the neuropsychological organisation of dreaming: implications for psychoanalysis. *Bulletin of the Anna Freud Centre, 16*: 149–166.

Solms, M. (1995). New findings on the neurological organisation of dreaming: implications for psychoanalysis. *Psychoanalytical Quarterly, 64*: 43–67.

Solms, M. (1996). Towards an anatomy of the unconscious. *Journal of Clinical Psychoanalysis, 5*: 332–367.

Solms, M. (1997). *The Neuropsychology of Dreams*. Hillsdale, NJ: Lawrence Erlbaum Associates.

Spence, D. P. (1994). *The Rhetorical Voice of Psychoanalysis*. London: Harvard.

Staerke, J. (1919). The reversal of the libido sign in delusions of persecution. *International Journal of Psycho-Analysis, 1*: 231–234.

Steiner, J. (1993). *Psychic Retreats*. London: Routledge.

Steiner, R. (1995). Hermeneutics or hermes-mess. *International Journal of Psycho-Analysis, 76*: 435–445.

Stengel, E. (1953). *Introduction to Freud's "On Aphasia"*. London: Imago.

Stern, D. N. (1985). *The Interpersonal World of the Infant: A View from Psychoanalysis and Developmental Psychology*. New York: Basic Books [reprinted London: Karnac Books, 1998].

Sterba, R. (1934). The fate of the ego in analytic therapy. *International Journal of Psycho-Analysis, 15*: 117–127.

Strachey, J. (1934). The nature of the therapeutic action of psychoanalysis. *International Journal of Psycho-Analysis, 15*: 127–159.

Sullivan, H. S. (1962). *Schizophrenia as a Human Process*. New York: Norton.

Tuckett, D. (1994). The conceptualisation and communication of clinical facts in psychoanalysis. *International Journal of Psycho-Analysis, 75:* 865–870.

Van Ophuijsen, J. H. (1920). On the origin of the feeling of persecution. *International Journal of Psycho-Analysis, 1:* 235–279.

Wallerstein, R. S. (1990). Psychoanalysis: the common ground. *International Journal of Psycho-Analysis, 71:* 3–20.

Winnicott, D. W. (1965). *The Maturational Processes and the Facilitating Environment.* London: Hogarth [reprinted London: Karnac Books, 1995].

Yorke, S. C. B. (1993). Freud, metapsychology and other matters: reflections on some recent books. *Bulletin of the Anna Freud Centre, 16:* 297–324.

Yorke, S. C. B. (1995). Clinical assessment and psychoanalytic theory: finding the meeting point. *Bulletin of the Anna Freud Centre, 18:* 211–235.

Yorke, S. C. B. (1996). Diagnoses in clinical practice: its relationship to psychoanalytic theory. *Psychoanalytic Study of the Child, 51:* 190–214.

Yorke, S. C. B., Wiseberg, S., & Freeman, T. (1989). *Development and Psychopathology.* New Haven, CT: Yale University Press.

INDEX

abaissement du niveau mental, 83
Abend, S. M., 148
Abraham, K., xiv, 64, 107, 130, 156
    theory of object love of, 88–99, 128,
        129
Abrams, S., 1
abreaction, 124
affects, role of in hysteria, 12–13
ageing, effects of, 121
    see also Alzheimer's disease;
        arteriosclerotic dementia
aggression, 76, 138
Alzheimer's disease, 47, 116, 154
amnesia, 30, 32, 123
    hysterical, 134
    infantile, 86
    twilight, 83
anal retentiveness, 136
anal sadism, 92, 129
analysis, resistance, 123–128, 138
analytic process, viability of, 139–
        148
Anna O., 123

anorexia nervosa, 50
anticathexis, 30
anxiety(ies):
    depressive, 96, 160
    hysteria, 5, 13, 19, 83, 84, 123, 125
    morbid, 76, 77, 78
    phobic, 82
    psychotic, 129
        infantile, 94
    separation, 139
    signal, xiv, 73
    theories of [Freud], xiv, 71–78
        economic, xiv
        first, 71, 73, 75, 76
        second, 75, 76
aphasia, 15, 32
Arieti, S., 157
Arlow, J., 116, 117, 118, 120
arteriosclerotic dementia, 47, 116,
        153, 154
attention, selective, 48, 114, 152, 153
autism, 84, 116
    schizophrenic, 142

autistic phenomena, 103, 104

Baker, R., 147
Balint, M., 1, 107, 133, 138, 146
basic fault [Balint], 138
Bernard, C., 12
Bibring, E., 95
Bion, W. R., xiv, 79, 84, 120, 131, 132, 143, 145
Bleuler, E., 11, 54, 84, 85, 96, 101, 115, 116, 120, 152
Bleuler, M., 50, 82, 118, 140
Bollas, C., 137
borderline states, 140, 143, 145, 147
brain syndromes, 3
Brenner, C., 116, 117, 118, 120
Breuer, J., 12, 13, 14, 123, 124, 154
British Psychoanalytical Society, object relations school of, 133–138

Cameron, J. L., 3
cannibalistic phantasies, 90
Caper, R., 2, 3
catalepsy, 51
"catastrophic reactions" [Goldstein], 48
cathexes, 31, 32, 33, 47, 68, 69, 70, 80, 107
    build-up of, 14
        and unpleasure, 16
    concept of, 18, 31–33
        and pleasure principle, 13–18
    ego, loss of, 143
    energic, withdrawal of, 22
    instinctual, 77, 119
    libidinal: see libidinal cathexes
    mobile, 18
        binding of, 13, 15, 16
    object, 67
    preconscious, 30
    withdrawal of, 23, 30
    see also anticathexis
Chapman, J., 153
character neuroses, 3, 4, 30, 44, 55, 60, 74, 102, 140, 146

Chertok, L., 2
child psychoanalysis, 159–160
    Kleinian theory of, 128–133
chronic brain syndrome, 116
chronicity, 5, 76, 120
    end states [Bleuler], 118
clinical examples:
    anxiety:
        clinical phenomena of, 73
        hysteria, and loss of potency, 74
    cathexes:
        mobile, and repression, 33–34
        and substitute formation, 16–17
    defensive (pathological) narcissism, 107–108
    delusional jealousy (delusion of infidelity), 56–57
    depression and self-criticism replaced by paranoia, 63–64
    free association, role of, 151–152
    homosexuality, male, analytic work with, 58–59
    identification:
        with lost loved object, 61–62
        and wish-fulfilment, 9–10
    manic–depressive psychoses, 95
    psychoses and delusions, 97–98
    repetition compulsion, self-punitive, 37–39
    repression, characteristics of, 19–21
    schizophrenia(s), hebephrenic–catatonic type, 7–8
    sexual instinct:
        reversal of, 60
        turning round upon the subject's self, 60–61
    speech content, patients', understanding [clinical example], 7–8
    substitution, 153–154
    transference phenomena, 44–46
    traumatic event, effects of, 34–37
    wish(es):
        delusions, in schizophrenia, 108
        embedded in dreams, 9
        -fulfilment, 6–7

conscience, 62, 65
consciousness:
    field of, 83–84
    as function of ego, 67
constipation, and object loss, 89, 90
conversion hysteria, 13, 22
Couch, A., 127
countercathexis, 22, 23
countertransference, 128, 132, 133,
        137, 147, 157
Critchley, M., 48

Dali, S., 8
Darwinian evolutionary concepts,
        15
death instinct, xiii, xiv, xv, 67–70, 76,
        79, 81, 85, 105, 109, 112, 113,
        119, 149
    and masochism, 41
    and repetition compulsion, 40–52
    and sadism, 41
    and self-preservative instinct, 41
    theory of [Freud], 50
decathexis–recathexis (restitutional)
        theory [Freud], 142–146
defence:
    analysis, technique of, 123–128
    concept of, 126–128
    and narcissistic object relations,
        107–109
    transference of [A. Freud], 127
delusional jealousy (delusion of
        infidelity), xiii, 55, 57, 66
    vs. healthy jealousy, 55
delusional phantasies, 101
delusional thinking, 118
delusions, 8, 14, 56–60, 96–98, 113,
        116, 117, 119, 121, 141, 142,
        145, 153
    grandiose, 16
    persecutory, 11, 16, 56, 60, 65, 76,
        77, 110, 129, 144, 154
    and phantasies, 17, 115
    schizophrenic, 96
    wishful, 11, 17, 51, 108, 118
        of chronicity, 120

dentition, infant's, and concept of
        oral sadism, 156
depersonalization, 44, 46, 140
depression, xiii, 23, 56, 62, 66, 89, 105,
        151
    manic–(depressive): *see* manic–
        depressive psychoses
depressive anxieties, 96, 160
depressive position, 94–96, 112, 118,
        136, 160
depressive state, 61–63, 66, 68–70, 89,
        90, 94, 126
    and guilt, 68
    and mourning, 78
derealization, 44, 56, 140
development, psychoanalytic
        theories of, 88–99
diarrhoea, and object loss, 89
displacement, 10, 67, 80, 85, 111, 119,
        151
double bookkeeping, 84
dream(s), *passim*
    analysis of, role of, 6, 157
    as clinical facts, 3
    interpretation of, 124
    neuropsychological studies of
        [Solms], 155–156
    and psychical wish-fulfilment, 5–
        11
    traumatic, 33, 39, 49
    and wish-fulfilment, 5
dual instinct theory, xiv
dynamic templates and rules of
        functioning [Sandler], 86
dynamic–economic theory of anxiety,
        17, 80
dysmorphophobia, xv, 2, 50, 140–147

economic theory of anxiety, xiv, 72,
        75, 77
    see also dynamic–economic theory
        of anxiety
Edelson, M., 150
ego, 53–70
    anti-libidinal, 93, 134
    central, 134

ego (*continued*)
  composition of, 53, 54
    theory of, 58
  critical agency within, 53
  fragmented, 117
  functions of, 66, 67
  -ideal, 65, 95
  instinct, 40, 42, 43, 52, 76
  libidinal, 40, 101, 107, 134
  organization, 83, 117, 118, 126
    and anxiety, 71
    vs. self, 81
  and sexual identification, xiii
  structural concept of: *see* structural
    theory
  and topographical system, 67
  unconscious, vs. repressed
    unconscious, 53
  undifferentiated state of, 116
Emde, R. N., 160
empathy failure [Kohut], 138
endopsychic object relations, 103,
    117, 118, 134–137, 143, 144
end states [Bleuler], 118
envy, 65, 74, 82, 96, 104, 109, 129–132,
    141–145, 160
epilepsy, 47, 154
erotomania, 55–60, 66, 76, 110, 111
  and unconscious homosexuality,
    57
erythrophobia, 143
evolution, theory of [Jackson], 16
exhibitionism, 59, 60, 61, 66, 98, 125
Ey, H., 111

Fairbairn, W. R. D., xiv, 1, 79–82, 85,
    87, 104, 105, 107
  developmental theories of, 92–99
  treatment techniques of, 133–138
Federn, P., 115, 121, 142
Feldman, M., 133
Fenichel, O., 127
Ferenczi, S., 92, 99, 127, 133, 146
fetishism, 85
field of consciousness, 83, 84
  lowering level of, 83

Fisher, C., 152
"Fixité du Milieu Interieur, La",
    [Bernard], 12
Flechsig, P. E., 54
free association, 45, 123, 124, 135, 149
  theory of, 151
Freeman, R. E., 141, 146, 156
Freeman, T., xii–xvi, 3, 48, 55, 57, 67,
    74, 96, 102, 103, 110, 111, 116,
    127, 141, 146, 152, 156
Freud, A., 102, 127, 159, 160
  concept of transference of defence
    of, 127
Freud, S., *passim*
  Beyond the Pleasure Principle, 31–52
  on death instinct and repetitive
    phenomena, xiii
  Ego and the Id, The, 54, 66, 79
  *Group Psychology and the Analysis
    of the Ego*, 53, 64, 65, 79
  "Inhibitions, Symptoms and
    Anxiety", 71
  "Instincts and Their Vicissitudes",
    53
  Interpretation of Dreams, The, 11,
    79
  later theoretical expositions of, 1,
    31–52
  metapsychological concepts of, 4
  "Mourning and Melancholia", 53,
    79
  "Narcissism, On", 53
  on narcissistic object relations, xv
  on nature of wishing, 14–16
  on free association, 124–125
  on resistance analysis, 123–128
  original theoretical expositions of,
    1
  on pathological narcissism, 107
  pleasure/unpleasure principle of,
    5–18
  "Schreber case", 53
  structural theory of, xiii, xiv, 126–
    127
  theories of anxiety of, xiv, 71–78
  theories of dreams of, xv

theory of mind of, 11–14
theory of repression of, 19–30
theory of superego of, 126
on therapeutic task, 125
on transference neuroses, 125–126
use of term "ego", 53
Fromm-Reichmann, F., 143
Frosch, J., 55, 151
functional psychoses, 3, 4, 102

Gathercole, C. E., 48
Glover, E., 107, 127, 128
Goldstein, K., 48
greed, 94, 96, 104, 131, 144, 160
    acquisitive, 144
        sexual, 82
    destructive, 134
    oral, 129
Greenson, R., 147
Groddeck, G., 67
Grotstein, J., 143
group psychology, xiii
Grunbaum, A., 148, 149
guilt, unconscious, 53, 126

Habermas, J., 2
hallucinations, 11, 14, 15, 97, 110, 116,
        118–121, 144, 154
    auditory, 115
    dream, 16
    dreams as, 10
    and object loss, 14
hallucinatory gratification, 79, 80
    theory of [Freud], 14
hate, origins of [Freud], 52
hebephrenic–catatonic
        schizophrenias, 7, 48, 101, 121,
        141, 151–153, 157
Heimann, P., 128
    on countertransference, 132–133
helplessness, 46, 72, 73, 75, 77, 108,
        109, 111, 120, 133
Holmstrom, R., 157
Holt, R. R., 4
homosexuality, 22, 50, 56–58, 66, 100,
        102, 110

unconscious, 55, 57, 65
    vs. manifest, 55
hormone therapy, effects of, 121
hypochondriasis, 143
hysteria, 5, 13, 19, 83, 84, 123, 125
    anxiety, 20, 22, 30, 31, 77
    and repression, 22
    conversion, 13, 22
    Freud's theory of, 13
    theoretical concepts behind, 12
hysterical neuroses, 19, 124, 125, 127
hysterical symptoms, formation of,
    theory of, 124

id, 67, 69, 72, 73, 78, 116, 127
    composition of, 54
    functions of, 66
    and life and death instincts, 67
    system unconscious, 67
idealizing transference: see
        transference, idealizing
identification, 7–10, 21, 24–26, 29, 45,
        58, 64–68, 82, 89, 101, 109, 143,
        147
    masculine, 57
    oedipal, 68
    processes of, xiii, 53, 55
    projective, 81, 93, 97, 103, 105, 112,
        117, 119, 130–133, 138
    secondary, 55
    sexual, xiii
"impairment of switching" vs.
        "compulsive repetition"
        [Luria], 48, 49
incorporation, oral: see oral
        incorporation
instinct(s):
    death: see death instinct
    dual theory of, 69, 70
    ego: see ego instinct
    first theory of [Freud], 40
    life: see life instinct
    self-preservative, 40, 41, 70
    sexual: see sexual instinct
    theory of [Freud], 40
instinctual regression, 68, 91

internalization, psychical: *see*
    psychical internalization
internalizations, transmuting, 139
International Psychoanalytical
    Association, 4
interpretation:
    role of, 134
    transference, 131, 135, 137
introjection, 64, 68, 89, 90, 93, 96, 103,
    143

Jackson, J. H., 16, 88, 111
Janet, P., 83, 84, 85, 123
jealousy, 8, 10, 141
    delusional: *see* delusional jealousy
Joseph, B., 146

Katan, M., 98, 111, 113, 116–119, 121
    metapsychological theory of, 121
Kells, B., 141, 146
Kernberg, O., 143
Klauber, J., 137
Klein, G. S., 152, 153
Klein, M., 1, 76, 79, 80, 81, 85, 87, 110,
    112, 113, 120, 136, 140, 143,
    156, 159
    developmental theories of, 92–99
    object relations theories of, xiv
    on narcissistic object relations, xv,
        109
    on schizoid mechanisms, xv
    theory of narcissism of, 103–105
    theory of rescue phantasies, 160
    theory of schizoid mechanisms,
        107
    treatment technique of, 128–133
kleptomania, 91
Knight, G., 143
Kohon, G., 133, 137
Kohut, H., 1, 79, 85, 87, 102, 110, 112,
    113, 137, 140
    on narcissistic object relations, xv
    theory of narcissistic object
        relations of, 105–107
    treatment techniques of, 138–139
Kretchmer, E., 82

libidinal cathexes, xv, 71, 75, 78, 88,
    101, 110, 143
libidinal hypercathexis of self, 111
libido:
    concept of, 101
    ego: *see* ego libido
    introversion of, 40
    narcissistic: *see* narcissistic libido
    theory, xv, 101, 107, 109, 110, 112
    withdrawal of, 40, 143
life instinct, xiv, 41–52, 67, 70, 76, 105
linking, attack on [Bion], 84
logical verbal thinking, as function of
    ego, 67
London, N., 120
Lucas, R., 140
Luria, A. R., 48, 49

manic defence, 82, 94, 96, 112, 130
manic–depressive psychoses, 3, 89–
    95
Martindale, B., xii–xvi
masochism, 41, 59
masturbatory phantasy(ies), 3, 20, 25,
    27, 29, 30, 47, 59, 60, 61, 86, 87,
    108, 111
McGhie, A., 3, 153
melancholia, 96
    and mourning, 78
memory(ies):
    of childhood sexual abuse, 86
    as function of ego, 67
mental apparatus, schema of [Freud],
    53–70
    new, 66–70
mental illness, signs of, 2
Milton, J., 32
mind, theory of:
    Freud's, 11–14, 31–52, 72, 157
    Klein's, 81
mirror transference: *see* transference,
    mirror
mother, role of in mental
    development, 92
motility, control of, as function of
    ego, 67

mourning, 78, 90, 96
multiple personality, 83

narcissism, xiii, 40, 87, 88, 103
    concept of, 100, 101
    destructive, 104, 105, 109, 110
        [Rosenfeld], 51
    infantile, 106
    libidinal, 105
    normal/healthy, 101
    pathological, xv, 101, 107, 109–113
        and narcissistic object relations,
            109–111
        secondary, 113
        theory of, 112–113
    pre-psychotic, 111
    primary, 101, 111, 113
    psychopathology of, 107
    psychotic, 111, 113
    secondary, 101, 109, 111, 113
    theory of, 105
        Klein's, 103
narcissistic libido, 41, 43, 68
    theory of abnormal development
        of, 112–113
narcissistic love object, 58
narcissistic object relations:
    and boundaries of self, 101–105
    as outcome of defence, 107–109
    and pathological narcissism, 109–
        111
    theories of, 100–113
        Freud's, xv, 112–113
        Klein's, xv, 112–113
        Kohut's, xv, 105–107, 112–113
negative therapeutic reaction, 68, 70,
    104, 126
negativism, 2, 50, 51, 97, 103, 117,
    136
neuroses, 9, 20, 21, 40, 54, 73, 76, 78,
    82, 125–127, 142, 147, 151, 157
    character: *see* character neuroses
    conflict theory of, 139
    hysterical: *see* hysterical neuroses
    obsessional: *see* obsessional
        neurosis

psychopathology of, and
    repression, 19
symptom: *see* symptom neuroses
symptom formation in, 125
transference: *see* transference
    neuroses
traumatic, 32–34, 39, 43–52, 72
treatment of, 141
Nirvana principle [Freud], 42
Nunberg, H., 102, 107

object:
    attacks on, 93
    part: *see* part object
    choice, 88
        heterosexual, 21
        identification based on, 58
        narcissistic, 58, 88, 100, 102, 110
        narcissistic homosexual, 57, 102
        regression from, 64
        replacement of, by
            identification, 67
    libido, theory of abnormal
        development of, 112–113
    love, 92, 107
        and auto-erotism, 88
        full, 92
        growth of, theory of, 89–99, 128
        loss of capacity for, 88
        partial, 91–92
    relations, 79, 98, 101
        endopsychic: *see* endopsychic
            object relations
    relations, narcissistic:
        hallmarks of, 106
        Kohut's theory of, 105–107
        omnipotent, 104
        theories of, 100–113
    school, of British Psychoanalytical
        Society, treatment techniques
        of, 133–138
    representation:
        and libidinal cathexes, 101, 103
        part object as first, 93, 99
        and self-representations, 102, 109
        splitting of, 80

obsessional neuroses, 5, 13, 19, 68–70, 89–92, 124, 125
  and guilt, 68
  vs. manic–depressive states, 89
Oedipus complex, 160
Ogden, T. H., 143
omnipotence, 80, 93, 94, 96, 98, 102, 104, 106, 108, 112, 118, 130, 131
"omnipotent narcissistic object relations" [Rosenfeld], 104
omnipotent phantasies, 23, 108, 109, 134
  reparative, 82, 119, 154
  sadistic, 82
  unconscious, 94
oral incorporation, 64, 93, 94
oral sadism, 93, 94, 156
oral–sadistic phantasies, 90, 91, 96, 156
  unconscious, 85
oral-sadism, 95
Orenstein, A., 2
Orenstein, P., 2
organic mental state(s), 1, 3, 4, 15, 55, 102, 115, 151, 152, 153
O'Shaughnessy, E., 2, 150

Pao, P. N., 116, 117, 118, 120
paranoia, 55, 77, 92, 142
  persecutory, 70, 88, 92, 99
paranoid–schizoid position, 94, 112, 117, 118, 146
parapraxes, xii, 3, 80
parathymia, 84
part object, 81, 91–95, 98–99
Payne, R. W., 115
perception, as function of ego, 67
perseveration, 47, 48
perseverative phenomena, 2, 48
personality, psychotic organizations of, 119
phantasy(ies):
  omnipotent: see omnipotent phantasies

oral–sadistic: see oral–sadistic phantasies
rescue, and child psychoanalysis, 159–160
unconscious: see unconscious phantasy
phase of restitution [Freud], 84
phobia formation, 77
phobic anxiety, 82
pleasure principle, xiii, 31, 69, 80, 155
  theory of, 5–18, 54, 67
Poetzl, O., 153
Porder, M. S., 148
preconscious cathexis, withdrawal of, 30
primal repression [Freud], 23–30
primary identification, 55
primary narcissism, 101, 111, 113
primary processes, xiii, xiv, 15, 66, 80, 81, 111, 116, 119
primary repression, 23, 30, 86
  and masturbatory phantasies, 23–30
"Principle of Constancy" [Freud], 12
projection, 47, 81, 93, 96, 97, 104, 109, 126, 131–133, 143
projective identification, 81, 93, 97, 103, 105, 112, 117, 119, 130–133, 137
Pruyser, P., 85
psychical internalization: see introjection
psychical structure, 85, 111, 116
psychical structures:
  and structural model, 80
  theory of, 68
psychopathogenesis, 118, 147
  theories of, 121, 123
    Abraham's, 92
    Balint's, 138
    Fairbairn's, 98–99, 138
    Klein's, 97–99
    Winnicott's, 138
psychopharmacological treatments, xv, 121

psychoses, *passim*
  acute, 55
  adult, xiv, 94
  functional, 3, 4, 102
  maniacal, 11
  manic, 116
    -depressive, 3, 50, 89
  paranoiac, 142
  paranoid, 65, 88, 94, 103, 113
  persecutory, 65, 94
  and psychoanalytic theories of
      development, 88–99
  role of death instinct in, 50–51
  schizophrenic, 10, 14, 37–40, 50, 54,
      76, 97, 102, 116, 118, 151
  transference, 145
psychotic phenomena:
  form of, theories of, 115–120
  formal aspects of, 114–122

"quota of affect" [Freud], 22, 75

Rank, O., 127
reaction formation, 126
reality testing, 62
  failure of, xv, 113, 119
  faults in, 47
  as function of ego, 67
reflective awareness, as function of
      ego, 67
regression, 89, 91, 116, 155
  instinctual: *see* instinctual
      regression
  libidinal, 89
  from object choice, 64
  temporal [Freud], 155
  topographic [Freud], 15, 16, 119,
      155
Reich, A., 128
Reik, T., 74
Reisenberg-Malcolm, R., 2
reparation, 82, 94, 96, 112, 118, 130
  omnipotent, 160
repetition compulsion, 34, 37, 39, 40,
      43, 47, 48, 49, 50

and pleasure principle, 39–42
repetitions, in transference, 44, 46, 49
repetitive phenomena, xiii, 34–39, 43,
      47–49, 87
repression, xiv, 31, 59, 65, 69, 72, 75,
      77, 84–86, 98, 126, 147, 149
  anxiety, 78
  failure of, 33
  as function of ego, 67
  lack of, 39
  primal, 86, 87
  primal [Freud], 23–30
  primary, 86
  theoretical concept of, origin of,
      19
  theory of, xiii, 19–30, 54, 86
rescue phantasies, and child
      psychoanalysis, 159–160
resistance, 149
  self-preservative aspect of, 128
  unconscious, 67, 126, 135
  analysis, 138
  technique of, 123–128
Ricoeur, P., 2
Roiphe, J., 150, 156
Rosenfeld, 51, 96, 103–105, 107, 109,
      110, 112, 120, 131, 132, 143

sadism, 60, 61, 68, 76, 95, 104, 109
  anal, 91, 92, 129
  and death instinct, 41–42
  masochism, 59
  oral, 93, 94, 156
Sandler, A. M., 2
Sandler, J., 2, 86, 128
Schafer, R., 2
Schilder, P., 48
Schimek, J. G., 124
schizoid mechanisms, 80–82, 97, 103–
      109, 112, 130–132, 143
  theory of [Klein], xv, 80, 110, 112–
      113, 136
  see also splitting
schizoid personality, 82, 83, 93, 105
  disorder, 82, 111–113

schizoid position, 93, 134
  [Fairbairn], 82, 138
schizophrenia(s), 3, 77, 91, 103, 104,
      113, 116, 131, 134, 140–143, 145
  non-remitting, 9, 11, 16, 17, 39, 49,
      108, 111, 120, 121, 141, 152
  hebephrenic–catatonic type, 7,
      48, 101, 121, 141, 151–153, 157
  paranoid, 65, 88, 94
  psychopathogenesis of, 118, 141
  symptomatology of, 97
  theory of:
    Bleuler's, 84
    Klein's, 143
schizophrenic delusions: see
      delusions, schizophrenic
schizophrenic psychoses: see
      psychoses, schizophrenic
Schreber, D. G. M., 54
  case, 53
scoptophilia, 21, 29, 59, 66, 98, 124
screen memories, 23, 87
Searles, H., 143
secondary gain, role of, 126
secondary identification, 55
secondary narcissism, 101, 109, 111,
      113
secondary processes, xiii, 15, 16, 31,
      33, 40, 47, 49, 66, 67, 69
secondary system, 69
Segal, H., 118
selective attention: see attention,
      selective
self, boundary of, and narcissistic
      object relations, 101–105
self–object relationships, 58
self-object, 106, 107, 139
  idealized, 138
  mirroring, 138
  parental, 138
self-preservation, instinct of, 40, 42
self-representation, vs. object
      representations: see object
      representation and self-
      representations

self-reproaches:
  in depressive states, 66, 89
    following object loss, 61, 63
  in manic–depressive states, 95
separation anxiety, 139
sexual identification, xiii
sexual instinct, 13, 40, 41, 59
  reversal of, 59
  turning round upon the subject's
      self, 59–61
Shevrin, H., 150
signal anxiety, xiv, 72, 73, 75, 77
Solms, M., 12, 13, 32, 155, 156
somnambulism, 83
Spence, D. P., 3, 150, 154
splitting, 93, 97, 99, 103–105, 112, 119,
      130, 131, 134–136
  of ego, 81, 85, 118
  psychical, concept of, xiv, 80–87
  systematic [Bleuler], 84
Staerke, J., 92, 99
Steiner, J., 109, 112, 119, 120, 145, 146
Steiner, R., 2, 150
Stengel, E., 16
Stengers, I., 2
Sterba, R., 147
Stern, D. N., 160
Stevenson, R. L., 152
structural theory [Freud], xiii, xiv, 18,
      53, 54–70, 76, 80–81, 126, 149
  antecedents of, 54–66
substitute formation, 5, 7, 11, 16, 22,
      80
substitution, 7, 151–154
  of object through self, 66, 111
  of self through object, 66
suggestibility, 137, 148, 156, 157
Sullivan, H. S., 143
superego, 68–73, 126–129, 139
  functioning, theory of [Freud], xiv,
      66
  and sexual identification, xiii
  structural concept of, 53
symptom neuroses, 1, 3, 4, 74, 125,
      126, 127, 134, 146

systematic splitting [Bleuler], 84

tachistoscopic experiments, 67
theory of mind, 13
thinking, "over-inclusive", 115
topographical regression, 15
transference, 24, 26, 34–36, 39, 46, 49,
    57, 117, 124–148
  analysis of, 157
  anxiety, 28
  concept of, 130
  –countertransference interaction,
    137
  eroticized (transference love), 57
  hate, 130
  idealizing, 106, 139
  interpretation: see interpretation,
    transference
  love, 57, 110
  mirror, 106, 139
  neuroses, 19, 22, 40, 43, 44, 125
    and repression, 21
  phantasies, 2
    unconscious, 145
  phenomena, 21, 45, 102, 104
  positive, 142, 143, 147
  psychosis, 145
  repetitions, 44, 46, 49
  and resistance, 125, 138
  thoughts, 35, 43, 114, 134
  unconscious, 128
    phantasies, 131
    psychotic, 145
  working, 55, 89, 95
transitivism, 38, 55, 66, 84, 101, 102,
    117, 141
transitivistic phenomena, 54, 96, 103,
    110, 115
traumatic event, effects of, 34–39

traumatic neuroses: see neuroses,
    traumatic
true and false self [Winnicott], 138
Tuckett, D., 150

unconscious, repressed, vs.
    unconscious ego, 53
unconscious phantasy, 79, 93, 98, 117,
    118, 119, 130, 145
undifferentiated state of ego, 118,
    119
  [Katan], 113, 116, 117

Van Ophuijsen, J. H., 92, 99
verification:
  necessity of, 150
  problem of, in psychoanalytic
    process, 2, 159, 160

Wallerstein, R. S., xv, 140, 147
Willick, M. S., 148
Winnicott, D. W., 1, 133, 138, 146
Wiseberg, S., 127
wish:
  -fulfilment, xiii, xiv, 14, 15, 16, 17,
    18, 31, 33, 42, 64, 66, 69, 80, 81,
    154
    psychical, and dreams, 5–11
  phantasies, 97, 102, 116
    adolescent, 3
    childhood, 87
    exhibitionistic, 57
    oral–sadistic, 156
    sexual, 124
    sexual sadistic, 21
wishing, 5, 9, 14, 42, 80, 153, 155
  nature of [Freud], 14–16

Yorke, S. C. B., 127, 149, 154, 160